elsbeth e
Sumeera Dawood
Lisemelo Tlale
Elizabeth Trew
Anet Kemp
Baitse Mokiti

Myesha Jenkins
Arja Salafranca
Makhosazana Xaba
Riana Wiechers
Bongekile Mbanjwa
Anna Anuradhá Varney

Photographs

Neo Ntsoma, Suzy Bernstein
Riana Wiechers, Anna Anuradhá Varney

Editor: Allan Kolski Horwitz

First published in 2005 by Botsotso Publishing
Box 30952 Braamfontein, 2017, South Africa
e-mail: botsotso@artslink.co.za

© in the text; the poets themselves
© in the photographs; the photographers themselves

ISBN: 0-620-34878-X

English translations of Bongekile Mbanjwa's poems; Siphiwe ka Ngwenya

Cover & text design & layout: Anna Anuradhá Varney

Some of these poems have been previously published in magazines such as Botsotso, Carapace, Fidelities, New Coin and Timbila. Should we have omitted any acknowledgements, please accept the publisher's apology.

Contents

Neo Ntsoma – Photographs   8-10

elsbeth e
Silence   11
A little town at a time . . .   12
The fairy godmother   14
In the haze of the Twins   15
The life and death of a Mineworker   16
Diorama on a Tuesday   17
(to Melanie Gossling who wrote the story)
Honna   18
'n Familie moord   19
Illusions   20
My cousin Gary   21
This poem should be untitled but it isn't . . . 22
Art   23
Domestic Worker blues in a reggae rhythm   24
Revolution   25
Asylums change over time   26

Suzy Bernstein – Photographs   27-29

Sumeera Dawood
Departure 11   31
Red Brick   32
Watermelon in my throat   33
A grade one at heart   34
8:42   35
Dominate me   36
Disillusionment   37
History needs my hand   38
Make me stay   39
(Untitled)   40
Secrets make us giddy   41
Desert   42
Your pretty face is going to hell   43
Again   44

Riana Wiechers – Photographs   45-47

Lisemelo Tlale
So long, dear   48
Silenced by psychosis and rage   49
The New Year waits for the four o'clock train   51
Hospital Bracelet stories: 'Eunice 1-5-1974'   52
The way I live my life   53
Experience at the Vagina Monologues   54
The dump, my refuge, my home   56
What makes the Self (Part 1)   57
That Swazi day   58
Moyo inferno   59
The Surreal display titled,
"And y'drew the Land, man"   60
Origins of Solitude   61
The Spoof of the Lucky woman
and her prowess   62
Moxton of yesteryear, Papa of today   63
A night so young   64
This Freewoman Land   65

Neo Ntsoma – Photographs   66-68

Elizabeth Trew
Gathering redness   69
Convent meal   70
Handwriting   71
A Norway tree   72
The rat house   74
Old country woman   75
Through the coastal trees   76
In Egypt   79
Musi's donga   84
Cave one   86

Suzy Bernstein – Photographs   87-89

Anet Kemp
Losing sight of the sun   90
sleeping beauty awakes   91
moon gift   92
insurection   93

exclaimmations   94
my black Alien with the most
beautiful pink Head   96
rumpelstilzkin   97
the moon was waning hcr hcart's bleeding day 98
queen of hearts   99
chaotic avoiDances: an enD story   100
eroties-gotiese reisverby Jupiter en beyond   102
'n reis getrek na die lyne in my hand   105
kantelkop   108
rooi 11   110
die groot val   112
hansel and gretel   114

Riana Wiechers – Photographs   115-117

Baitse Mokiti
That's me   118
Morning   119
The Boys In My Life   120
Daifern   121
The Slaughter of The Innocents   122
Someday   123
Growing Tired   124
For My Other   125
Unwritten   126
Writer's Block – Blank Thoughts On Lined Paper
– 22.5cm x 16.5cm   127

Neo Ntsoma – Photographs   128-130

Myesha Jenkins
The nature of me   131
Autobiography   132
Mother   134
Anticipation   135
The launch   136
Heritage   137
Jazz music   138
Kids   140
Makwapeni   142
Animal   143
Creatures of the night   144

Suzy Bernstein – Photographs   145-147

Arja Salafranca
We reach out   149
A woman selecting cleaning fluids   151
Another day   152
Kissing the wall   153
Foreign ice   154
On the trains   156
The elephant is unhappy   157
The monk meditates   158
Medieval face   160

Neo Ntsoma – Photographs   161-163

Makhosazana Xaba
Waking up   164
Farting knees: talking to myself   165
Views of my Cancerian friends   166
Trivia holds   168
Mornings on weekdays   169
Wishing   170
Locked   172
Skin Speak   173
Find me a fan   174
My book   175
This dance   176

Photographs – Riana Wiechers   177-179

Riana Wiechers
first resolution   181
Vrydagaand 6:47pm   182
Dis oukei   183
Mr fearful   184
kyk baby   185
hart tot maag   186
tonight I will   187
klein drakies   188
look at me   189
siamese seisoene   190
dans (soos ek nou)   191
Valium and fireballs   192
wat's 'n afrikaner   193

Suzy Bernstein – Photographs   194-196

Bongekile Margaret Mbanjwa
English translations – Siphiwe ka Ngwenya
Isihluthulelo   198
Translation – Lock and key   199
Kungenxa kabani   200
Translation – Whose fault is it?   201
Uzozo   202
Translation – The Shack   203
Kanti kungani   204
Translation – Why?   205
Uzifozonke   206
Translation – The Plague   207

Riana Wiechers – Photographs   208-210

Anna Anuradhá Varney
Alchemy   211
For Gra-anna   212
Measured   213
End of a cycle   214
Sea Point   215
Divine Kali   216
There is no choice   217
Sacred Yoni   218
A piece of jazz   219
Notes written on the train in Mossel Bay   220
Prayer   221
Selection   222

Anna Anuradhá Varney – Photographs
                                             223-225

Biographies   226

Botsotso Publishing Titles   228

elsbeth e

Silence

unless she wants to collapse
under the burden of keeping
life and death apart
she must
Breathe

A little town at a time . . .

I know too many small towns from the inside out.
I know.
No one really knows how many people live there. They don't count the
bodies in that place. It is not important. They know how many graves are
marked and how many not. How many people left and how many stayed.
And those who are yet to be born they leave to the hands of the rubbing old
women and knowing gods for they have their own ways that few can
recognize and most must fear. Here every thing has its place and for some
nothing has it's time. At this place, washing hangs because it must on days
when the wind blows strong.
There.
They know enough… how many houses there are, whose child was fathered
by which man on what day of which season, who sees in the burning
playfulness of the sun revenge from a living God, which woman needs to be
watched carefully, whose clothes needs to be passed down to whom.
There.
Small towns live in two minds. It's back turned to that which it cannot
change and that which their own eyes cannot believe. I know. I come
from there.
I was born there. I return now. To small places.

Every other week I pack my bags and I go. Back.

On gravel roads cutting away the skin of distance, carving me back into
what ought to be… a little town at a time. But it cannot be the same.
I speak with a pausing tongue for the things I have to say are strange and
out of place.
Development.

A secluded word that falls too easily off my mother's tongue and puts out
the fire between them and me. Us. They who are black and rural like me,
makes me walk in mourning with a bowed head and closed eyes swaying
dangerously like a thirsty child towards tears. Here. Learned knowledge
loses its certainty and the mind is tripped like a circle drawn violently in
the air given belief by the nod of a passing stranger.

For

they know what time it was when the world stopped and stared and moved on leaving it's name behind in the starving bark of a dog chasing leaves. Here the world waits and redeems itself in the name of dogs who answer to Bin Laden, Pagad, Mandela... Here. Dogs, who are seldom called, seldom touched, often chased away and mostly fed with the shame of left over meatless bones are the memory of a world gone forgotten. Here. Dogs are a white smile and a black scream. They are explained in time. Never understood with time.

It is here.

That they know they give birth to me every time I return. They know.

And I know.

That I must know my place.

The fairy godmother

The juice of dried out sweet thorns rolled over her tongue
was also the keepsake of the head of a praying mantis pinched off
she laid both out on the back of her hand
and sang out loud yes jesus loves you
goats chased to the mouth of the dry river bed
was bare feet on the edge of quicksand
flirting dangerously with the sign that said keep out
this the place where they the ones who love to play
made Belief stand on her head
and swear that Boesman was not her daddy
and this place was not a sin and a shame

On her way home she heard of shuffling feet
stoning butchers grown ups shaking heads
the constable thrusting curses into the wind
he was with Joey's mother who cleaned the cells
when they came to tell
about Swing and his eye
his shame was the mark on his pants
holding the moment of his fall in seconds that didn't know it was part of
time
before he said let the man come to me
I drive after no brown arse whoring drunk
Girlie was a child struck by grief
her daddy's eye was cut with a screw
at the corner of Sing a long
She left the fairy godmother behind
pulling what she knew of him to her there in the middle of nowhere
sweets daddy, hole in the middle lifesavers
iim sitting cross legged
eyes closed like a holy man she didn't know
She turned away from housing truths covered her mouth
with the back of her hand
and never spoke words like love bread and family again

In the haze of the Twins

a thousand truths will crawl on the back
of what was
and we will all find meaning
on the scattered limps
of what is now –
and what has always been
a nation united by a barefaced lie:
all is well in the land of the free

The life and death of a Mineworker

All those years he overheard his mother
When you dig up earth it should be to measure the weight of the world
He did not understand
He did not listen
His mother did not know the weight of light and dark
In his eighteen year old world
As he went deeper and deeper and deeper
his ears thinned and collapsed
inside the open womb of the earth
As he dreams

Between boys from Carolusberg and their black words
who watched him grow old fighting reasons to age gracefully
while defending everything he has lost
inside the act of being broken by the gap between his teeth
He dreams of leaving this place

His flesh spreads like daisy seeds blown by an August wind
He becomes a handful of dirt
He settles on gravel and falling rocks
He knows the dreadful beating of his mother's chest
Will seek escape behind a cup of tea
And it will be luck that leads the gravedigger's song
away from his mother's tears
Someone will say lets pray before he lose his soul just like his Father

Diorama on a Tuesday
(to Melanie Gossling who wrote the story)

I cannot see I cannot feel Tuesday grieving
Over how many bodies burned in ovens
Remains don't stay behind on the palms of those cleaning ash
The man over the phone said that that Diorama is Our holocaust
It is there on black and white that he is San
                              Without inverted commas
His people are spoken for
In a paper that he would most probably never read

I look again at this picture before me
It was after all nothing but a small scene
with three-dimensional figures
a man squatting arrow and bow another standing up
one two three four women and child
capturing a moment in passing
bodies cut out in stares their own and those from the outside looking in

I assume she is white they mostly are
This woman who mourns the casting of casts
She repeats Her words have no echo
Naked and still in The Times
I must believe
This is the way we want to be remembered
Breathing bodies fit into molds
In a place that weighs dust over time

Honna

She rose
The sound a sniff
Her body shaking
Before the heaviness on her chest
Can become a catch in her throat

She rises her head walking off the man's list while she stands
Skeletons he slept with made love with fucked
All monsters to ease the disease become a smear
Her tears blurring the smell of him
Maggots living inside her heart killing him
Her body stands tall
"that a girl" it must be the old man who saw her first steps
Towards the frame

This thing exploding inside her
Burning her fingers is not the reason why she rose
Not knowing whether the other women were alive
was not the small comfort he thought would be enough
to make her stay hating them with him
Wait for the figs
another season
summer maybe
he will make it if

She touched an odd feeling
the young them smiling behind glass
Their love a frame falling out of her hands breaking
She turned to him and said, I hate you

'n Familie moord

Korreltjie droom druk haar voos
Haar man is broos
Sy naam is Koos
Die nood van haar kroos
Druk hom boos
Nou lê sy in 'n doos
Sy en haar kroos
Saam met Koos
Korreltjie droom loop nou vors
Sonder dors of broodjie kors

Illusions

Children of slaves
Tell them you Knew
The raingiver
The wounded knee
The evening sun
The mercy of dawn
The song of silence
Before God
The holy book
The cross
The hymns
The guilt
You were in awe of
The infinite one

My cousin Gary

He was...
Always searching for himself in the wrong faces
His dead sister
His disapproving mother
His silent father
He was...
Always feeding from the wrong places
The middle of Station Road
A bench in the park
An empty jar of assorted cookies
The end of a beggars chain
He was...
Always missing from himself
A tear in a faded shirt
A fifty cents under a shoe in a mosque
A knot in my heart
He is...
Dead now

This poem should be untitled but it isn't...

June 2001. It is a cold night in the Cederberg. Diane and I are showing the movie "Once were warriors", a story depicting its own truths about the life of the Maoris in New Zealand. As the man hits his wife, boys ranging from the ages of 14 – 18 shout in screaming laughter, "Hit her, hit her". The same happens when the 13 year old girl is raped by her uncle.
I am tired.

"Once were warriors"
My tongue is a floating egg
It cannot lock my ears to the cold darkness outside

Or the barren song in the eyes of these almost men
Who sing together an aged old howl
Their christian names a chosen whisper now
In this same place between the altar the cross
They will come for Sundays prayers...

It comes from within
Deep
Too deep for me to know from where
And how?
How a cry for war rolling free in a screaming laughter can run so lost
so fast?

How familiar is this place that it can hold such anger?

So many of us here
are growing in short rough edges of silence
While you drive home your hate
On the breath of my skin
You strangle your warriors cry
Hit her hit her hit her

Art

I will continue to live in the dark
Draw words over broken glass with the soles of my feet
For you have already baptized it pain
And for that you could lose yourself in the tangles
Of why and when and how
But we can both pretend that it rings a false note
Somewhere
In the rubbish of our minds
And play with the inside of our hands all a long the sickly sweet smell of
lies flying
Above mismatched side-plates
And questions left unanswered
I will continue to live in the dark
Draw words over broken glass with the soles of my feet

Domestic worker blues in a reggae rhythm

Sugar on bread
Ah water from a t t tap
Down a black child's belly
Down a black child's belly
Who think jelly is only for white Sally
With the curls and the dress with the frills
But her mamma is gonna come
Her mamma is gonna come
With plastic bags that shags
What's all this jazz
Hunger carries only one flag
Sugar on bread
Ah water from a t t tap
Down a black child's belly
Down a black child's belly
Look that woman
Who sells her fanny to Danny and many
Five kids without Dick
Ain't that sick how we all lick
When there ain't much to pick
Sugar on bread
Ah water from a t t tap
Down a black
Down a black child
Down a black child's belly
Who waits Cause her momma's gonna come

Revolution

They forgot

The wars they fought

Ran through burning streets

Lifted arms over their heads

Threw stones at guns

Africa

Risked a t-shirt print

Freedom

They make so many decisions

With unclenched fists

Fat fingers

On paper and napkins

Africa

At war

With a game of snakes and ladders

Blood grows on diamonds

For this
They say
Children died

Asylums change over time
(for Kabelo)

fucked by missing cat's eyes on the road in broad day light
you misplaced your memory like a second helping

in wrapped foil on the table that freaked out balance
while you talked about unforgiving madness

the phrased words of long gone angry ones smeared on four walls
the dead eyes of the absent ones who gave you pills on the hour
your back capturing solace in the shade of streams of toilet paper

Asylums change over time
You said
which ambushed the Undertaker on a quiet day
pushing the smell of yesterdays cremation on all fours
you survived
never to be the same again

Sumeera Dawood

.... This watermelon is tough
A street fighter
It puts up quite a defence:
Up down left right it bobs
Hurls itself against constraints
Trying to sidestep the tensed muscles
And seize a gap ....

Departure II

I remember the old wives' tales.
Silly thing to remember about your childhood.
Talk of the ocean coming back to claim the land
And bad luck finding the salt spiller.

I thought of you and walked to the kitchen
And tossed that salt out. All of it.
The jar perpendicular to the floor.

You're leaving.
I told you to.

Your space constricts like gum
swiftly accommodating for the loss of a tooth.
The tightening muscle eats away the vacant space
As a worm would an apple.

I think of you sometimes
And my thawing popsicle eyes tell me how much I miss you.
Wasted moment.
Wasted tears.
After all this time, the ocean still has not claimed its land.

Red Brick

So many things have been inside me.
Old Mr Wilschird's fingers, Sol's tongue
And Naddie.
I want to close my thighs,
The spanner arms of my metal soul.

I'll close my legs.
I'll get up from toilet seats and hotel floors.
Whore. Slut. Immoral. Whatever.
I'm tired.

My heart is a red, red brick:
Used as a veranda doorstop.
Used as a line marker in children's hopscotch games.
Used as a flowerbed border.
Used as a braai grid holster.
Used and used

And splintered.

One day
Red powder will attach itself to air
to light
and fly.

Watermelon in my throat

Clenched tongue
Clenched throat
Clenched shoulders
Clenched heart
Corner a watermelon in my windpipe.

This watermelon is tough
A street fighter
It puts up quite a defence:
Up down left right it bobs
Hurls itself against constraints
Trying to sidestep the tensed muscles
And seize a gap.

It's only when Eyes with its notorious drive-by tendencies unleashes a rain
of
t e a r s that everyone steps away.

A grade-one at heart

He told me to read.
So I put down my comic
And decoded his eyes.
"I don't understand the words," I said.

Thump! He threw a dictionary into my lap.
A squirt from the eye, an ejaculation:
One eyebrow arched, he issued the unspoken challenge.

I slumped down and flipped the book open
And closed my eyes to the shape and colour of the words,
And listened

To the electric buzz permeating through the curtains
And his tight little jockey.

8:42

The bathroom's the loneliness room

Your eyes are dull in the mirror's reflection
Like dirty broken glass bits that need one finger
wipe to shimmer. You're finding it hard not to look
away. You're elsewhere, you've gone off with
your thoughts and what's-her-name
Passion
and left me alone. I'm always alone
when you touch me.

Dominate me

Take me by the heart and cure me of my evil, evil, evil ways.
Look me in the eye and slyly, smoothly, steal my will from me.
Yank those paper-like words from my mouth, hand and head forever.
Dominate me; leave me with no choice at all.
That, that knowledge – oppressive knowledge – cruelly sneaks up on me,
Conditioning me into a state of numbness: clearly I know too much.

Except for those gratifyingly lifeless moments
When you find your way around the maze of my brain,

Flicking the "off" button.

Dominate me.

Disillusionment

Crunching into the core of my arm
he bit
and held on
to the flesh between his teeth.
I always thought the penis contained a bone.

With my teeth I searched
amongst the node-like flesh
but none were found.
A dog without her bone:
I choose for him to reduce me to.

A green-blue-brown ring now on my arm resides.
A ring, solid and unending
that weans me off its pearly shine.
Fading slowly.
Slowly.

History needs my hand

I used to be six,
I used to stare up at the sky,
Totally amazed when I realised the complexity of life.
I used to get a hiding with a silly-fore
And I used to cry in the separate toilet outside.

I used to have a pair of red Elephants – so ugly bright red
That they spurred on the fire within me, my sense of justice.
I used to think that I was lonely, and alone in the world –
And I would bemoan my fate,
Until I consciously decided to violate my aloneness,
Albeit it not a true violation.

I used to see the world in black and white frames,
And then when the simplistically naïve world I constructed vanished,
Shades of grey introduced themselves.
I stopped talking to trees.

I used to cry with a boy called Ayaz.
I did not know who he was,
Until he revealed himself to be just another man,
An ordinary man, malleable and without strength.
I used to be loved by a father whose love could not be contained
And who saw me as a beautiful, beautiful woman.

I used to see myself as a girl,
Because that's the way I acted.
One day I was self-powerless and lived in Cravenby Street on Earth,
And the next day I did not.

I flipped the page.

Make me stay

I'll leave you
And you will not know it.
I am like that.

I'll leave you
Midfuck
While my body grabs hold of you with its elastic walls.

Have I already left you?
It happens so fast:
My mind's eye wanders
Up the skirts of firm legs
And lingers there a while.

(Untitled)

Muslim boys and their vows
of no penetration. There's nothing better
than religious guilt to heat things up
a bit. His bit bobs
inside my mouth. I don't move on the toilet seat,
motionless like an ocean-watcher before the ebb
and flow. Bobs
as I mock-gag. Bobs
as I watch the city sky melt
like make-up on a hot day. Pink, orange
hues of yellow and then royal blue. Dripping
swirling together. Nice enough
for a toilet seat view.

He's brown and warm
like a hollow Easter egg. My fingers stretch
through the soft chocolate and into air. Grasping
nothing. Grasping everything.

Secrets make us giddy

Raj's secret makes him giddy.
He holds it inside of him
and it scrapes against his stomach
as it does its somersaults.

Raj feels it as butterfly kicks:
gracious and fluid in movement.

The Breasts look on jealously,
Froth-mouthed and sullen with expectation.

Oblivious, Raj holds his secret close to him.
It makes him giddy.

The desert

Barefoot, allowing the scorching sand to swoosh through my toes,
I walk aimlessly.
My nose belies my eyes:
In the endless heaps of flyaway sand,
All I can smell is the stingingly salty smell of the ocean.
The ocean, with its Time-stifling ebb and flow;
The ebb that slips off my skin,
The flow that washes my insides clean.
But now, before this desert, this mighty desert
Whose sand clings to my skin, scaling over me,
I stand totally numb.
Paralysed by the sticky molten that hides between the sand,
That makes my fury boil and boil and spit
No more
And renders me pliant.

Your pretty face is going to hell

Your pretty face
is going to hell
Elusivemyass
You're cold and fashionably bland
A frozen chicken on a conveyor belt
two seconds away from plastic packaging.

I thought I could save you
yes you know the story
Perhapsvanityismymiddlename
I placed my lips firmly on yours
and swirled around your tongue
as children do ice-cream cones.

But I loved the splinters
of unbearably tender moments with you
theywouldmakemybreastsburn
My voice was that of a taxi guardtjie
Loud incessant tones, alien tongue
His Kep-Town-Be-hel-villes were my I-love-yous.

And then it was over
Over in the sense that I told you off
thisisntworkinganymore
You walked on
I was left with my decision,
an ever-present piece of glass in my foam flip-flop.

Again

The next time I lay down on cold bathroom tiles it will be for
Love.

The next time I realize that I don't want to, I will get up.
The next time, I will voice my objection.

Floating driftwood.
Sometimes I feel like a piece of driftwood in this large pond:
i land.

i hurt me again.
i hurt me so terribly again.

My mother has me on my knees.

Requiem for Monday.
Requiem for happiness.

Carrot centres, caramel, blisters and glass cuts, scarfs, blonde hair and
freckles.
When will this cycle ever end?

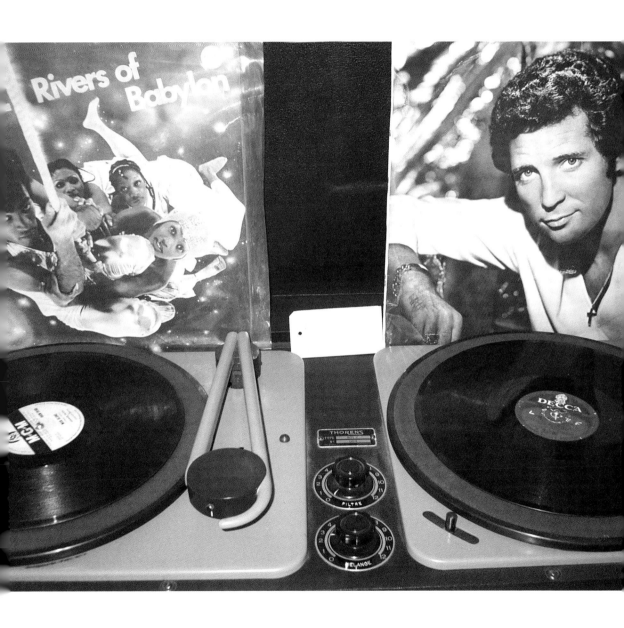

Lisemelo Jlale

So long, dear

I am tired of walking this straight line:
I need some reckless reason to limp away
from this wreckage with wounds to be proud of.
I could worry them with my drinking, or perhaps
promiscuity, or even suicidal tendencies. I think I will
shock them with a wedding band and perhaps some
morning sickness. Maybe suggestively touch a
stranger on a bus. Maybe, just maybe, stop
feeling guilty for being alive ... the natural
course of Life is not this! Or maybe it is.

Silenced by psychosis and rage

So if I have all these dreams and guts to do anything and everything I desire, why was I sitting on my couch crying like a woman who has just lost a child? I blame it all on a circumstance, of the dramatic kind. I have buried my anger and pain, far too deep. Once it was Kolya, now it is The House of Sand and Fog. When does it end?
The forces of nature were at work. The time was right. The context was perfect.

I was scared that someone who did not bring me into this world, threatened to take me out – without my permission. But was it this that caused the sudden, almost-violent disturbance in my mind and in my heart? It was Cause-and-effect.
Cause and effect of the Kingsley rendition of my father's road labour and attempted degradations at the hands of pale ignorance. Cause is fear. Effect is betrayal of the lesser kind; perhaps, dancing is my only way out. I told you this was drama!

I scoffed down a slice of strawberry cheesecake. I looked in the mirror and the flab and anorexic magazine life made me question my Faith! How dare they claim to know about loneliness! I forgave because bitterness does not suit me. But the pent up energy knocked on my door – this was a desperate need to smash someone's skull in! I should rinse the ring left by shock and age out my cup.

I dressed and faked it like the Conservative Party because the world is still not friendly to single travellers. In a fit of rage I jumped out of a plane at 30,000 ft to feel the forceful wind against my chubby cheeks. While freefalling at a tremendous speed, I held out my hand to my Maker. Back to one of those infamous couch rests, I felt my world crumbling. Such is drama: Act 1.

I love it when I surpass my petrol attendant's expectations –
the look in his eyes knows about compassion. Thence tis not pity.
I love my mother. I love my sister.
I love my brothers. I love my country.
I love the sound of rain against my bedroom window, especially slow rain, on a Sunday morning.
I am in love with my Fate – she gave me reason to live.

The smug Pretenders at work whispered out their own weaknesses,
I yelled out like an Amazon that I am labelled, "Race card is not about
declared trumps!" They totally disregarded my identity, heritage and Pain.
They saw my mother's boldness as utter disrespect towards the Patriarchy;
my siblings and I saw a persistent pioneer who opened not only mental but
intellectual doors for us.
Hacking away at this negative publicity can be distracting: Please remind me
to look up to verify my bearings.

These are smirks of earth after rain downpours and sun shiny smiles, it is
the smell of hot peanut butter rye toast and roasted coffee beans – it is safe,
it is sane. While my people tend to their crude shelters in the thick of
things, they flee to their holiday cabins. Yesterday they spit on my great
grandfather. Today he must beg them to reconcile their oppressive falsehood
and pardoned arrogance.
When did they ask for forgiveness, granddaddy?

You have to admit, Africa's curves are bewitching. The continent is worth
the trouble, I mean, the travel.

I bawled my eyes because I was scared to scream for Help. So help me.

The New Year waits for the four o'clock train

I toiled without betterment, and persisted to no avail. The excuses left me exhausted.

While others comment, "This summer must be the hottest yet!" I nod a silent: "It is hotter." We observe and ignore these symptoms, every cycle. I observed the harsh realities of grief. And ignored the Need to reassure loved ones of my sanity and well-being. It is true I caught the cyclical bug.

I decided to tune into my desires by listening to the inner Self's creative urges. There was a voice that whispered words of negativity and failure, but now my soul's true voice is inspiring these images of success and sweet Expression. There is nothing like a Zero hour to get one to wake up! My year has been like a small lab experiment – an explosion here and a discovery there. Predictably, the results and the reactions were unforeseen – even with the calculated hypotheses. Gorecki was a common catalyst in this year's concoction of laziness, self-doubt and of course, Awakening of Cesaria's Sabine Largam! Art or Science? Definitely, scientific Art. Art in the form of a Sacred Cow. The art is Alive and Colourful. The art questions preconception and expresses Freedom to challenge the status quo.

While others' cows have lost weight and tanned, mine glides into the new Calendar a happily rounded babe. Will yours be lazing and sitting on a park bench with a newspaper in hand? Will she protest against the Pamplona Bull Run? Will she be in shimmery lipgloss and stiletto heels? Will she be with child?

The art is a Legacy and hence about evolved culture. The art answers the Earth's prayers and seeks to clarify Nouveau art.

While others' cows closed deals in torn jeans and an attitude, mine dried her eyes and now waits for the four o'clock train. The "inner calf" in my cow is smiling. She is terrified. She is hopeful of her new Invention.

My love for Life has been rekindled.

Hospital Bracelet stories: 'Eunice 1-5-1974'

Her story,
 a healthy baby was borne on this day, to me. An adult whose immune foundation was built
 on an experimental vita-mined Pill. Dr Mokhesi declared the elusive pregnancy a miracle.
 She gained the name, "Certificate", she was all I earned for an aided semester
 lost to her rearing. Her very perfect pink, long fingers far surpassed the nightlong
 labour suffering. We left the Parys hospital to face the inquisitive
 audience. Paternal, or Maternal? Lisemelo, or Moroesi? She left the hospital 'Baby Eunice
 1-5-1974' and months later my beautiful Afro'ed bundle was named, Lisemelo Moroesi
 Jacqueline. For one expected at the end of April, I had neatly packed her layette, complete
 with two vests, two pairs of booties, two kappies, a shawl, a blankie. I was ready for her arrival.

My story,
 the doctor prophesied my defence system would kick the habitual vita-min indulgence; and
 true enough, the long fingered self sold her chubby Afro for the spiritual locks:
 these Seriti my mother passed on to me. Paternally strong or maternally talented? This
 truly was a heavy burden to carry for one so young! What is in a name? My names attract the Sun.
 I could point out the attention was welcomed, even as I feared the stolen cheek pinches
 by those who call themselves aunties! Names ranged from 'Wami, ou swaer to the ever merciful
 lisped version of Moroesi. Twenty-nine years later, I am still in awe of the hospital baby bracelet that identified this newborn. The miracle here was, my mother returned
 to her full-time studies for her merited Certificates. Today, she is packing her boots to
 join me for a cold, wet Cape winter. Once more, it will be just the two of us. I am ready for her arrival.

The way I live my life

the duly birth set me on a path of dirty tactics –
of course the jazz queen would sail her dinghy
into an array of dilemma; past the shebeen where
a shilling is worth the igloo i would plant my
roots in; now, as the ice queen i had my friends
in the audience – the women in crimson tights
whilst the men were clad in jaded dungarees –
wondering if i would live to my namesake's
intelligence, humility, and great powerful
stature – but I would bow out at the end of the
show a Gypsy with a smile on my face.

Experience at the Vagina Monologues

The first night of every period, every month, of every year
I would drift into an eternal
   hell, where I do not know
Who I am
How could I when I deny
    What makes the Self?
    Shame,
    Anger, definitely
    Sadness
My monologues? These do not
include Pleasure, Contentment; no bidet for me!
This prologue is sadly about
    Pain,
    Blood, maybe
    Shame
This daily lament over what-could-have-been begs to question
if the above could Help to
    Re-visit,
    Re-pair, perhaps
    Re-habilitate
Those of us whose Ignorance
is excused because of Innocence, or even Social traps? The penalty is
    Abandonment,
    Slavery, even
    Death
Yes Disappointing! The sickening hypocrisy of Press freedom
silencing my self-inflicted misery? I am not one to
    Nag,
    Offend, or even
    Betray
Today I am honoured with the
a chance to hold my hand mirror
    Proudly,
    Boldly, maybe
    Rightfully so!
I am not Madonna, nor am I Cassandra Wilson; I
cannot claim comfort with the Self, especially with my Anatomy!
   Live,

Life, or
Survive?
Never! From now on This Woman's destiny lies with a
Hand Mirror,
the Self – and
down There?

The dump, my refuge, my home

Twas not paradise, but, had all that the Garden of Eden was.
Do not be fooled by the Elizabethan architecture of the driveway. The landscape had many in awe. This –
Impressionist painting had even I, in dire need to experience its Life.
The trip to my haven started on a Dark, Loud note where I was to find my Utopia.
There it was, marked solidly – 105!
The welcoming vile odour, seemed so aromatic. This was the smell I'd have to acquaint myself with. This was my new home.
My new home had a large room logically separated for my
Convenience, and so what if the plumbing was of Medieval Age?
Vermin was the order of the day, or should I say, the year?
What view? The ruckus from the street was sufficient
to get even a 'reasonable man' to write a bestseller! I had a pet, in fact, a number of pets.
Oh, these were friendly neighbours; twas their cats I had a problem with. This was my new home.
I know. Hardly a place to entertain friends – where were they? However distasteful my crib sounds twas this place that saw me a grown woman. This place was my refuge, my home after the Storm. Twas at this rendezvous, I met Life.

What makes the Self? (Part I)

Moroesi, Nthwesa,'Wami, Seme, Wittes, jazzie,
Mo, Lis; the list is infinite. Names of far away places,
across borders and seas – you think? The names are me – all me.
Symbolizing the many stages through the ages of my existence.
As
a
little girl,
I would see adults' dreams turn into my reality. I would
learn about pain. I would experience men's wrath.
I would be taught about women's displaced anger.
I learnt that
life does not revolve around me.
As
a
teenage girl,
I would see my family's implied loyalty. I would
learn about being Black, traditions and culture. I would
experience a white man's ignorant cruelty. I would be
taught about a white woman's displaced anger.
I learnt that
as a Black child, I was on my own.
As
a
young woman,
I would see distant lands. I would learn about co-existence
and tolerance. I would experience friendship and compassion.
I would be taught about a man's impatience and a
woman's displaced anger.
I learnt that
I have to understand to be understood.
As
a
woman,
I am seeing and realising some of my dreams. I am learning
about my passions and desires. I am experiencing wonder.
I am being taught about love and the "thinnest slice that
do not count for much".
I am learning.

That Swazi day

we set off to bulumba, on the barberton side of laughter
and rage – the tiresome low budget criminal account of
padre amaro led to sin: slap chips and umbrella cocktails
over chip gambling. Swazi News reported that Swazis are
Drunks, this could explain the suicidal pup en route to
jeppe's reef border. given the status quo, I'd also
take my chances with the jeep's bumper.

Moyo inferno

Twas truly a beautiful evening, twas the African make-up that spoke of European street beggars of the 18th century. We were all dressed to the Nines. The stunning conductor's Strength was bent out of shape by the Rhythm and Rhyme of Carmen's tempo. He felt it, and filled us with the excitement of the two-year-old on a hot summer's ice-cream drip-drop Day. He played with my unkempt Afro locks, and sat beside me on the chilled, steel seats under the Oak tree that Keanu's sickened Love brought with it a fine morning. The vineyard butterfly rescue of the grape crop was synonymous with the carnal dance performed by the Preying Mantis masochists. Twas foggy, and warm, and all too bright! The ground coffee ground the enthused footsteps of an Old English couple. This was their 21st century life, but were they really reliving their 20th? They were so in Love. Hand in hand, they led each other to the Land of sticky strawberries, crunchy pines and soothing Rain – this was a beginning of yet another day in their Heaven, on Earth. Others sought attention, by saving a hapless grasshopper, in the midst of hungry holidaymakers. What is that about, honestly Sean?

The night was about the sipping of pure water, the silky tart, the fresh melon, and the tangy mushroom: the mussel called me Owami. Twas the beautiful African sunset that kept us apart and yet, that which led us to meet, again. Dimpho di Kopane, and indeed they were, made me do silly things; I felt all tingly and warm inside. I galloped about, chewed on mint leaves, and screamed obscenities at the uppity Austrian aristocracy. The acorn fell, the Oak tree fell, and I fell in Love with the defunct carriage that used to be pulled by stallions. Now an auction piece, tis displayed as an ornamental piece for show – signifying the Life that was. Twas truly a 17th century night, filled with Passion, Energy and Love. We loved the music. We loved its Past and its Promise. And that is why I wrote this for you.

The Surreal display titled, "And y'drew the Land, man"

my heart pulsates in all directions; the throbs are Loud
Louder than my breathing – so Loud
she Blows me a kiss, and causes a sea storm, and
then asks me to take his hand!
he Shines in the dark, like the desert high noon; that is what his
smiles are to me – rare de-lights
my long toes cast prints on the wet sandy beach, and
each step excites the liver; i believe the puffed-up clouds
are here to see me – to see the tears run down my face
the Plan here is to accept Love, unconditionally
 i touched her face and found safety in the coldness of her nose –
    I lay on top of him and put my ear against
    his chest; his heart beat faster and faster
    Pulse to pulse. Breath to breath.
    We are one now.
    The wonder here is that All my fears disappeared.
    "Even grown-ups make mistakes", I concluded.
 i held his hands in mine and felt the kindness in their softness
my test was to accept the Self, unconditionally
i run my fingers through his hair, the dead-growths
feel like stretched-out arms of a happy childhood
i believe the hooter, the siren and the wails are echoes of Knowledge –
for me to hear; And to listen to the Pleas of the Pacifiers
he Whispers in the wind, winding a sand storm, as
he calls onto my unsuspecting heart; this time,
her humble bovine eye winks a "Chin up!", and
sends ripples on the still banks of my dream lake
my heart pulsates in all directions, the throbs are Loud
Louder than my breathing – so Loud

Origins of Solitude

My stellar friends greet the stillness of the night. They hide their starry eyes behind the protective clouds as I reach my hand out to touch their brightness. Then Eeyore loses his tail just as I am reminded of that Verve bloke whose friend did not make it – the drugs did not work, in fact, they made things worse, I hear. I am fatalist.

Earlier, the promenade stroll ended with a breather on a wooden chair as I looked out onto the vast blue waters. A silver-eyed mutt and I came face-to-face in a moment of truth: He stared asking: why the long face, my Nubian sister?

He seemed content with a nod and a smile for then he went about his way. Still mystified by the keen-eyed Messenger, I felt a strange sensation above my upper lip – the Birth of a massive 'vry puisie':

Who could have a crush on this cynic?

Later on, I witnessed another bumblebee massacre – when does it end?
Two weeks before I witnessed one writhing in pain to its last minutes alive.
Days ago, a beheaded brawny bee lay on the curb.

Pooh and Piglet go hunting? Good night all.

The Spoof of the Lucky woman and her prowess

Swing it Flavoured skinhead boy – that's right,
one, 3,5 and turn! Why it is your "lily white ass"
questions the Inevitable is beyond Clarity! Just
believe, in doubt, ask Oortjies, the Rottweiler!
The pink Elephant is not the oddity she is here
to Liberate us, boo – you ask if is this a Privilege? Perhaps.
Meanwhile, how about it Dancing King: Show off your fancy
footwork and tell me about this thing you call Love –
I promise to whip that nose into Shape,
for one day you will Rock another's knickers:
Joni Mitchell sings it – don't it All just seem to go
and you do not know what you have till it's gone.

Moxton of yesteryear, Papa of today

With an umbrella, you not only sheltered me from the rain, your soaked jersey
signified a selfless sacrifice that is honoured whenever filth
wipe their noses on mine.

Your ineffable humane presence astounded many. Talent for comedy is bestowed to the
very fortunate few; I believe 'twas Prophet Mohammed who uttered, "He deserves Paradise
who makes his companions laugh."

When I pointed out your boldness and "influential tongue" to the World, I
sought to express how great an orator you are. You brazenly moved forward to not
only make a Life for yourself but a name a father would be proud of.

Old man,
I am aware of ignorant rant and raves of those who believe themselves to
be deities. I wish you were in Kashiefaland, to tender to my wounded heart. Perhaps
concoct your infamous home remedies to Save our Souls ...

Do not mistake my drive and need for independence as being disrespectful;
I
am Living your Mother's path. I would have loved to have fulfilled the
organic farm dream... but age, oh age, how I wish!

How I wish you to meet your granddaughter – for you to read
to her "Ali Baba and the 40 Thieves"; Perhaps even quote Henry Wadsworth Longfellow's
"Osseo and Oweenee", after all, 'all its splendour is in language':
to harness the Appreciation and Love for the narrative art form!

Ou swaer,
let me pour tea for us; we'll show promise to the family tree prophesy and I
could explain my brusque manner at the Vereeniging branch – 'twas my first day's work, papa!
Strong with a touch of sweetness: That is my father.

A night so young ...

"Hashish?" Or maybe a lascivious lyric for the cancan,
as background music? A ditty evolved from a laden proposal,
by the lake named after honey, Tupelo honey to be exact.
I floated lackadaisically into a scarlet vacuum, where
a yarmulke or a yashmak was a fashion nobility. The
Madhatters exposed the Temptress Inquisition. The Time will come. I hope
then I will know what to do. Dizzy? No, I said my name is Lisemelo.

This Freewoman Land

Basking in Respect, my heritage did not come with a curfew, only careful
groveling insured my heroine status. My peers' apathy lent this hoyden's life
Tiresome.
I had nothing to lose: the opposite was complaisance, and I am not Plain.

The saga continues.
A cul-de-sac? Bodice? Where is the hose? I am a bonsai. I have deep roots.
Look at me as I reach out my hands as if to fly – ornamental?
No, perhaps mini, but no less firm. I am a Brahmin. I am a nomad,
brash but not arrogant. I know I will bow out of this phase
a Gypsy with a smile on my face.

I am talking about Passion for the less obvious and the forgotten.
A 'Non-disclosure' clause is an understatement:
we talk about implied Loyalty and Support, where Beauty is a
smooth, white breast of a gull as it prepares for lift-off; and
Imagination is the alchemy of polarizing Life into an inanimate Image,
wow!
Freedom is a state of being sound inside – a visible Impression to the
Outside world.

I am talking about Living life that is good for the Soul –
not always rosy, very pleasant, considering
I am sometimes an impudent African woman with a very, very sweet tooth.

Elizabeth Trew

Gathering redness

I am gathering redness,
not receding cool reds
but deep passionfed bloodlines
of poppy and plum and star-wounds of pointsettia
inflamed fusions of burnt-orange suns
outrageous rubies on terracotta.
I am wheeling revolutions
through the puffed language of royals
to the wail of red sirens;

an exile writes about home in red ink
on pages sweet as coconut milk
wet with his blood

a woman dances inside her red city
a burning voice in the arms of her windmill
a ruby tear in her navel

an orphan remembers lifting the cup
to terracotta lips.
She is sewing a memory cloth, joining red squares
threading cowries, bead letters
and the delicate whorl of her mother's ear.

Into the spiraling dance of full-bodied redness,
not my pale thinning reds
but leaping towards the internal flame
the arrowroot of gold
its fierce closeness, its weighty dilating birth
the attention of love.

Convent meal

Today
Mother Superior
presides at high table.
Solid in habitual black she
graces the food,
sits and eyes
tranquilly
whorls of girls in drifting blue – tender
petals of profusion whose
transient faces
hover above the brisket
eddying high sound
as the waterjug passes.

While she,
over bread pudding
ever smiling
enquiring
sinks teeth, smooth ivory notes
vigorously
into the sweet.

Later
we rise to more prayer,
her girls dispersing into hazy sky
of their outside court
flying fine hair and bones between the bells.

While she,
highest mother of the house
swings heavy robes through
hallowed corridors of days –
perpetually.

Handwriting

Touching you –
soles of your feet, palms of your hands
scars on your tough, battered face
from your head-on crash

the time they found you alive in the morgue
when they re-set nose, cheekbone and jaw
stitched back your skin
your head held in place by a cage

Sis! somebody said to you in your cage
Beauty and the Beast, my mother said
Go for plastic surgery, your mother begged

choosing instead a far country, snowcapped
to mend post-office mailbags   alone
A blackbird sang to me all summer long, you said

Back home on your head sunburn imprinted on skin
mending mailbags again   revolutionary
jailbird in the courtyard jail

when I caught your first tear behind soundless glass
in the visitor's room
our country apart in a cage

Writing to me from your cell
I dreamed of your tear and your head
beginning to heal

Unwrapping your gift –
tough builder's hands, the flight of birds
song of your chest   sheen of your back
your modest, miraculous head

dovetailing
raisinsweet   salt –
decades mending skin

A Norway tree

Once, to my father's tundra place
far north of the southern cape
I sat in a wooden prow
in my scarlet riding coat.
I sailed along the deepest fjord
by mossy feet of the precipice.
Tree-roots clung to ice-scarred rock and
branches floated past.
High above a herd of reindeer
crossed the snow.
All left their long reflections in the boat
on the glassy sea below.

Along wide water rich fishing grounds and
fertile banks of peach and plum where
folded grass hung out to dry.
All my north kin by their inlet sea
leaned out to me.
I clutched the leaves of my other tongue
as Johanna shyly showed me in.
A feast of fish and breads on the rose embroidery, and
on wooden walls all the faces of my solemn kin.
That night I tossed in a wooden cot in another sky
in the tail of the midnight sun.

Folk came to meet his youngest child and
told me the tale of Olaf's son with the golden eye
who long ago had sailed away
to Africa's southern Cape
while the village church bell rang.
Everywhere my father's face
on every table fish and bread and
in the darkest evergreen
soft falling trees,
the piercing grind of someone sawing wood

as I heard my father's saw-mill
in the valley at the Cape.

Once we reached the fjord's snout
Alfred, in his dark-blue Sunday suit
pushed out his boat to grandmother's place
on the other mountain side.
He rowed across with a plash of oars
facing me in my blood red coat
as I trailed my hand in milk-blue waves
by the little fishing boat.

Alfred rowed to the lapping edge.
We walked past folded hay and
my father's hut.
Along the path a blond horse cropped the grass
crows flew to the trees above
as I ran to her and
saw my startled face in hers.
Farmor* sat in a heavy shawl
her long hair knotted and tied.
Many times she cried out
clasping the daughter of her long-lost son.
Velkommen, Olafsdatter, kom!
Velkommen, Olafsdatter, kom!

farmor – father's mother

73

The rat house

You were constantly mothering
closed in your house, housing – call it Loss.
I too was locked in, nursing Harm.

Did that whiskery gentleman
unbutton his tweeds, his breath popping
around your neck, his body filling your house?

Did you swell with bodies and tiny feet
kicking to come out, soon to give
multiple birth?

Soon you had your hands full
putting out bowls of warmed milk
and tenderized meats for your children

who ran amok in the lounge oiling the furniture
munching biscuits and flour in the kitchen
racing up and down passage and stairs.

The stillborn kept in a jar
the newborns asleep in a drawer
the two who played in a shoe.

When they took you out pleading
"My babies, don't take them away!"
I could finally meet you.

Old country woman

Old woman drives out the herd
on the hills of midsummer
moves lithe as a girl to the hooves and the bells

Old woman beds down under stone
calling her flock by the clattering stream
mutters a dream to the midnight sun

Old woman pours milk, boiling blood
by the fire
opens a caul to bring in a child's cry

Old woman spins, folding wings
of a shawl
treading the loom and refolding the cloth

Ancient girl sucking her cheeks
peeping out moonstruck
peels the rind of the sun

listening, listening

Through the coastal trees

I kept asking where are you, souls
of the dead. Where are you, the young ones
who are missing, where are you,
the completely transformed?

Adam Zagajewski. (In May)

and we sang
in praise of those who journey
those who found the way

Edward Brathwaite. (The Forest)

Away from the inland plantation we meet tonight's thunder
at the edge of our country. Our only vision is offshore
flashes of light – dolphin swimmers in phosphorus, and
in trees glow-worms beginning.
At the door of the storm we walk across stones

you are the voices in stones laid down on the slave coast

as bones ground and leached

as the mill crushing grain

as the floor lit silver and gold from your ship of trees

as music in stones knocking like dice

the founders

Above Africa's ocean we pull towards forest.
Silent dark gates, soaring crowns,
green eclipses of sun.
Nothing stirs but lianas left hanging

you are high as the sun rising over the sea on indigenous trees

as hearts hanging on blackwood and milkwood

as bows tilted and tuned

as masts keeping sail

as rows of lianas – phantom limbs

you wait as retainers

Daylight dazzles the green canopy.
We move single file on tables of leafbone
treading small movements underfoot

you are the fertile movement of ground-swell

in leaves falling to peat-musk

in the sweetness of humus

in roots bedding and branching

in seeds pushing pods open

the earth-makers

Saplings grow beside parent woods.
Small fists appear at the feet of mother trees,
old beard covers the canopy while
suckers and climbers cling to their hosts,
limbs stretching tree to tree.
We struggle through blades, hostile thicket

you are new warriors and host of the strangler

children sown into violence

the bells on death rows

the fists open and closed

the blades' rise and fall

you are warriors beginning

From our tunnel of thorns oozing sick light
we hear sounds of a stream and rush to fill bags with sweet water

you are vessels of balm washing wounds of all travellers

as the breeze on a stream

as cups running over

as lilies of peace

as dew in spring

you repair the soiled tunnel, the peace-makers

Between light and dark we cross sentries of immigrant trees
through silent leaf fall in the rise and fall chain of hills.

Down a steep headland breathing in forest chambers –
crimson cells and gold-shafted mansions
beside cries and whispers, tongues set in darkness

you dwell in the chain many mouths of a kingdom

as the water-snake flees, slipping into its rainbow

as the song-bird flies, dropping silent red feathers

as the webbed spider spins, turning her wheel

as honey-bees hum across lime-scented trees

eyes and ears of the forest, inhabitors

Out of our forest the way opens.
Against a dark sun we drag small bags of water
past ribs of a boat on white sand

you remain to the left of a stream that once ran to the sea

the heart's lodge on its stem

the eye of a sphinx

the gull's wishbone

the snake slipping down reaching water

you remain as the witnesses

We have reached green sugarbush, a swift river,
bending down to the river-mouth turbulence,
the thundering place between river and sea.
Into the wide knocking throat
into needle-rock teeth we have come
to the river-rush meeting.
As swimmers crossing the rising confluence
we, the receivers, approach and are altered
through the forest beloved, beginning

In Egypt

1

The Nile has come from the south
drifts along her dry valley, stretches north
threads and ties carpet weave to her alluvial backbone
sews roots of date palm between clover and cotton
in her workbasket bundles of bulrush, papyrus

she floats barges of sugar cane
rafts of water rose
fills earthen jars
lifts the shadouf, the felucca
unravels washing past water buffalo

her swirl broadens and curves among villages
glides between leaves of rock
crouched hills, buildings
sways and slips through her padlocks

her old blood stirs over a drowned girl
a discarded factory boiler
she frets through the city

languid lady mends rips in her skin
at her elbow opens the lotus
silts her delta and slowly disrobes

always cording the spring out of earth
in another country,
the bubbling African child
the rush of cataract twins
flowing shoulder to shoulder, butting the mother

2

Leaving the Old Kingdom five thousand years back
Noot's body lifted and rose from the earth.
Her body became great.
Living in heaven she became powerful, immortal
becoming the sacred sky goddess
who floated above her worshipping people.

Each dawn in the east she swallowed the sun
to begin a new solar hymn.
Each evening she bled in the west
when the sun seeped through her legs.
Each night in sequins her dark body
bit into the moon.

Lovely Noot keeping active aerobic
stretched across Egypt to reach her horizon.
She could leap north to south of the Nile
in one long-legged leap.
She was seen upside down turning cartwheels.
She moved head over heels speeding light
or curled into a sandstorm.
Sucking navel to spine she would bend backwards
vaulting her belly to land a flip jump.
Times when she bathed like a lake in her fountain,
her blue body reaching overland
down to a girl brewing beer for a king.

Old sky mother Noot who shifting found gravity
willed the last hymn to her daughter:
Sacrifice your power
Go down and inherit the earth
Become mortal, merciful, just.

3

It is the desert queen Hatshepsut
whose face in disguise bears the marks of a king:
she wears the king's wig,
his beard cups her soft chin,
on her brow the king's cobra raises his head.
She is carved as a sphinx in local alabaster
her claws relaxed on their sandy plinth.
Desert winds have bitten one paw and flank
though her tail intact curls round her rump.
This was the popular perfumed queen who fetched
cargoes of incense trees from the gulf
for her fragrant scent garden.

But who is this woman
who parades a gilt collar and hips,
who holds a beauty contest in front of the sphinx?
Her headband holds tumbled black locks,
stiletto heels spike the dust.
This morning she left Cleopatra's Perfumery
at the edge of the city
smelling of Lotus and Desert Secret
mingled with feral scent.
Sunglasses cover her kohl-blackened lids.
Her feet ache. She kicks off her shoes,
curls her back and sits on the cool rump.

4

She enters the night under the bridge
the girl selling nuts
below Cairo's neon and ruby-lit roar
under her hood
her face lit from the coals
in her dustbin brazier
night after night muffled in smoke
she rumbles hot groundnuts and sunflower seeds
into her scoop
under the bridge in her dark
thundering corner
the nut girl
the owl girl feathered in smoke
glows under her hood
her unblinking glass eye in the night

5

All night in the monastery I hear winter winds,
ragged pilgrims, blowing stiff and cold
across desert, brittle as the moon.
Winds thirsting the red sea.
Winds murmuring like holy hermits
moving into their mountain sanctuary.
Winds howling and running like wolves over bones.
Winds humming in the bell tower.
Winds in the east wing, the deep choir
and chant of angel bars which soar in the cloisters.
Long breaths of wind with the wail
of cats in the pilgrims' quarter,
where a wind creeps into our cell
and lies beside Bertha asleep.

Littlewinds bask, new kittens in the sun.
Bertha, dressed in black for the monk
rotates her lame leg towards the guest room.
Last night's dream spun her wild arabic dervish,
a winding bride of the monastery
shaking her gold tambourine.
A gold disc shines above the monk's head.
A wisp of celestial breath lies on his tongue,
slides down his beard
and lands besides Bertha, kissing her foot.

Small winds lap stones in the watergarden,
ruffle cats in the courtyard,
frisk a monk meditating, secluded in his tree.
Small winds stretching tall
wave with the monk to Bertha and me.

Down from the monastery migrating winds
race with the minibus along the red coast.
Flags from the petrol plant fly
along pipes of oil bolted to stone.
Winds simmer, inflamed.
Winds of the desert sprouting new ribs of the world
spin fields of steel windmills,
winds sleek and laden with oil and the sea's breath.

Littlewinds drift, embalmed by the sea.
Soft winds puff Bertha's long hair
where she swings herself over stones
on the way to the breakwater
Hardly a sound as the nightwatchman smokes
outside a mansion blowing haloes to the sky.
Only a wind rattles the shutters, begging to come in.

Musi's donga
i.m. Fanuel Musi

Laid in your donga of earth
stones and soil fill your apron and mouth.
I sit by thatching grass
in our boundary of poplars and ash
sisal each side of the village path
with our two willows – the basket and weeping
between mealies and beans, among almond and peach

When the storm raged, ripping up ground
rains beating, breaking away earth
floods churning, sweeping down soils
you wept on the hill in two dongas scoured deep:
dry broken mouths   empty hearts

sixteen summers bowed alone across dongas
lifting your leather apron full of stones:
sifting stones   collecting stones   carting stones
nesting stones   walling stones
channeling rain   stemming rain
collecting silt   cradling silt
bridging and earthing

autumns winters gathering and rooting
gentling dung and ash in
binding soil in
swarding grass in
tilling seeds in
terracing
releasing piping the spring

sunrises sunsets taking
bread and tea down
working sweet passion on:
nights holding trembling hands

rubbing in aloe jelly
washing calluses and cuts
washing coloured soils and Lesotho dust

You lie soft in this earth
stones and soil filling apron and mouth
our grandson and son working on.
I sit in my harvest dress
red bishop-birds trill in the thatching grass
your heart in your donga of earth
and in mine.

Cave One
Sterkfontein

In this ancient dry territory, once lush riverine
bones and teeth are the seeds hold in iron-red earth
where we sweep for remains of huge monkeys and cats
and the hunting hyaena, and
where not long ago Dr Broom found the unbroken skull
of a girl he named Mrs Ples.

On the deepening shaft I bend into the warm sac of darkness
once full of water chiseling the stone elephant chamber
and a mother and child.

Here is a shaft where the young Mrs Ples
threw down her chewed hunting bones
into fossil-red breccia.
Down in furred water a gold hunter
called Hendrik sank into a rock-pool
and broke open his skull.

So I find you, small brown bat, cupped asleep,
beating warm blood
on the crystalline ear of the elephant,
your wing wrapped round a teat and a tiny heart.
I call you Petra, and hold you in my gaze
for a moment or two.

Coming up to the opening daylight heads
cast in bronze
move into view at the mouth of the cave.
I stroke the skull of Mrs Ples
and pinch the nose of Dr Broom
whose hand gently holds her for ever.

Anet Kemp

losing sight of the sun

we go our ways
disappear into the night
have dreams
but get wrinkles
we fight the flow inside
fuck swear at
our in-securities
we look at
our selves in mirrors and outside
and nothing exists
what we do paint write
are but traces closer to silence
and before silence
in between now and Silence
are whispers
haunting fearful cynical strokes
angry words jumping
like a pack of dogs
and we fear
we are about to give
the unforgivable

sleeping beauty awakes

sleeping beauty lies curled
waiting for her lover's hands
to wake her from her night's sleep

sleeping beauty feels him
slipping securely into her, opens
her sleepy eyes with a salacious smile

sleeping beauty presses her body into his
feels his hands gliding around
his fingers playing her pain

sleeping beauty's body awakes
dancing, she throws her head
towards the heavens

preys upon the sunlight calling
– she breaths deeply and screams the ecstasy
of his morning's glorious greeting

*It is desire itself that disseminates in a system of infinite deferral, copying the
vanishing point of perspective.*

Your	*[direct deferral of truth]*
Be	*[in absence forever lost to its mean ing]*
tray	*[break-fast handed on a pewter platter]*
all	*[ways and for eve r]*
Hits	*[the side of the face]*
Me	*[to whom knowledge of awakenings come]*
In	*[avoi dance]*
The	*[one One]*
Back	*[hanging on the washing line, like un send tex t]*

moon gift

I write love poems like a slave
they stream from me
into gutters
and when I am really inspired
I write for the man in the moon
who parks in a street
knocks on my door at ten to ten
and, with a cup of berry tea and peach schnapps
sits cross-legged on my bed
the man who knows my body
my weaknesses   strengths
    thoughts   rhythm

believe me   now   I am a strange angel
I don't miss his strange gifts
not his words dream-walking
    his presence on our soul wall
beloved reader, tell him I don't miss him
not those hands touching the mediocre other
nor that induced love
I don't miss him
tell him I've lost
 the 'keep-it-light'
one moonlit night
on the tail of a silver kite

I lie on my bed in the room with the black curtains
and white candles
under metal constructions
suspended from the ceiling
I lie naked in my long, purple fairy-coat
touch, but I don't miss him
so tell him, tell my lover with his full moon dreams
love does not tell of red heARTts
it is stolen hours in the wind
love is a hot oven, a sweat factory
a camel e-xperience without a single embrace
tell him hope is a burden
and my love wasted on a clean page
clean   semenclean

insurection

this night has no end
words follow like stones
in a stoned dream
of being the moon witch unighting
with the angel of trees
of being chased
by a beast into the forest
of dying in his vibrant hands
of being strangled
by a smooth cock
circling my neck
: snake waiting
to be worn
skintight
      making
x-es
     between
          my
legs
of being watched by a
god high up in a tree
calling me to come
up to follow
Him

till death do us part

exclaimmations

we can go
into psychologicalspiritual or ration all
            ex plan
                      nations
for the rise of the stars
for the brightness all around

we can throw our heads back
      calling the echo in caves
we can swim naked in the sea
make love under full moon rites
we can look into our peaks
    with lightning
        falling
        erect
  patterns in the sky
 and say yes
good
        timing
chaotic rhyming

we can proclaim: look at me
I'm a paper bark in the
              sky
      reaching
      immortality
with long green lushy fingers
we can create a lover's discourse
with Barthes announcing:
'The full moon this fall,
all night long
I have paced around the pond'

: throw your heads back, yes
he says softly as the stream flows
    : scream
      the edges of mountains
under the full moon winter shore

for I am there
                    here
every where
: nothing will ever throw me
                    again

my black Alien with the most beautiful pink Head

midnight sits on my white bed
brainstorm you through me
to leave us behind in words

in times when I should have been with you
I throw fashion shows in front of my mirror
trying to see me through your eyes

my awakening is a confused morning dream
with yoga positions in a backstreet hall
lights in unexpected corners

and security measures of which the source cannot be traced
I stand in my short school hockey skirt in front of a mirror
you say I have beautiful legs

the lights dim   we lie in wondrous shadows
in front of a blind through which the sun falls
in a large mirror I kiss THE SOURCE

on whom black paint cracks
I wash Him with gold in my fingers
until He sails Pink into my mouth

where I play His golden Cord
before He paints me red inside
and in The Eye of a Camera connects our enigmatic Birth

rumpelstilzkin

rumpelstizkin dances in the dark forest
rumpelstilzkin dances his name in the moonlit forest
rumpelstilzkin dances for the man in the moon a name
that will make him an accomplice
in the endless realisation
of A station
without a
name

What does rumpelstilzkin know about fairy tales? About saying too much? Once upon a time he was. And in our deepest secrets and losses he still is. He will always be there at the edge of your vision. A veil to remind you of a constant state of desire turned towards the past. Every time you close your eyes and touch yourself you will see a perfekt being flooding your body and soul with a reality brighter than your life. And if you listen closely you will hear the name under the veil. Rumpelstilzkin has many faces but only one is the One. The one you will see when you dare look too closely.

the moon was waning her heart's bleeding day

it was full moon on a good friday
and we miscarried it
instead an untimely monday ascended onto us
a bloody period

spiced up in a white tent
spaced out underneath the virgin veil
with the ship hovering faintly above the ceiling
we waited for the misconception

predicted by the night
dancing the witches dance
alone outside in moonlit winter garden
with naked warm body craving her love's touch

after such a lonely day of desires unfulfilled
the night was floating on a recognition
of being embraced in a world
where hiding is nothing

but a game lovers play underneath that virgin veil
where predictive echos bounce the chaos of discovery
covering his cock kissing her mouth
into that bleeding future

queen of hearts

shall I write to you, beloved
about love or war
shall I tell you about death
or do you want a fairy tale
and shall I spell out the setting
shall I lay bare the state of mind
in my cynical heart in my arty room
in my whacko, colour-rich house
in a wet, overgrown garden
that looks after itself
in a tropical, average-sized city

shall I say to you like antjie krog
'i am
god knows
a free fuckin' woman'
who knows what she wants
from a trembling man
hidden in his middle-class house in grey street

condemn me thus, beloved reader, condemn my guts
condemn my womanhood my romantic heart
because I want his everything
his house /in flames\ and his hands and his heart
condemn me violently, shave off my hair
beat me with a castigating whip
over my golden, supple back
scar my breasts
tighten my legs in chains
and burn the seed in my body on a stake

because I am a witch
beloved whore of his desire

chaotic avoiDances : an enD story

I was to a-void certain words
but they creep back
through dark alleys
they stream through treachery
scream from grave dreams
from behind burglar bars
from inside filled containers
chaos keeps on creeping
it hides in the seams of black curtains
in the flair of fairy dresses
swirling colours in the wind
in yellow files on desiring screen
behind screensavers
blocking the exits
of worlds in the whirl-
pool top loading washing
machine's cold caress

they beam through love's penetrating rites
as I walk a way
through the silent tunnel || in preclusion
as one side of my body burns
the other shakes from the tumble
I swift into unreal tournaments
a ghost warrior with a sword
knowing the one who enters
the forest too soon
destroys you surrounds your heart
between the layers of textured dresses over
Chinese lettering forming unknown
words on naked bodies
purple sunlight at your doorstep

                ☆☆☆

the further I fight
the sentence on its road in liberation
the moon's white lie

the more complicated becomes the structure
the more I crave the movement of my pen
its total immersion into the freedom
of unison   complete overthrow

☆☆☆

as I stand looking at white balloons
popping around my head
I erase the metal bird with one gaze
I erase the red bed in the red room
I erase the angel falling through the blinds
the glowing of summer's nerve ends
the dream in the violin string's vibration

hey you, come stand by me
one lastime || lasting time
I want you to feel the flying immortality
the bubbles of sensuality
in the sculpting sky so you will know
if I write about pain it is only to feed the summer sunrise
if I bleed it is to show where your fingers may follow
if I scream it is an invitation to dream
if I touch it is to heal the space of avoidance

until I am unable to see /////in/////terms/////of erasure:
two people lie naked on a bed the one is dead

*On twenty-five October in forest clouds repeating time the loved one
confirms to me that death is a word, life and pure energy the driving
force behind it. I saw through a window into infinity. Two people lie
naked on a bed, One more alive than all other...*

Eroties-gotiese reis verby Jupiter en beyond

die woorde wat ek teruglees klink
vreemd hees op my tong
soos ek gebeure verlore goedere
terugherlei na hul stasie
maar die sprong raak te amper aan die hemel
om gemaklik mee te verkeer

'ek gaan aan my woorde werk'
      '...my woorde bewerk'
      '... my woorde wek'
val die moontlikhede uit 'n hoë boom
voor my voete neer vloei dit stroomop
in die see van sewe strome
terwyl ek op die blou sylyn wat die hoofstroom oopvlek
myself saam op die kleur balanseer
waar energie vloei
en letters oor 'n skerm
, hande oor die landskap van die liefde

::die landskap van die liefde het wonder
baarlike heuwels teksture
en visuele bewonderingsreise vloei daaroor
soos selekantvisse in 'n stroom
//terwyl ek my skakelbord speel
asof ek die mees oorspronklike
klanke uit die klavier optower
//terwyl hy sy bas voor my uitstuur sekuur
//terwyl ek vorentoe tuur my hande soekend
aan sy growwe tekstuur

die uur is besig om oor te loop in sy arms
aan sy geheime lyf met die reuk van bas en sederolie
verloor ek my verbeelding
die klanke speel die melodieë deur my woorde
ek gee my oor aan die oggenddroom
aan die bloed in sy are
wat deur my mane stroom:

'ruik aan my hande, dit ruik na die seder aan jou lyf',
sê ek vir die donker man 'ruik aan my rug
waar die engelvlerke bloei' 'ruik aan my borste
waar jou hande roosblare groei' 'ruik aan my bene
waar benzoe lenig lê' 'ruik aan my arms
wat jou woudstorms omhels' en 'ruik aan my dye
waar jou soepel sonlyf my maan binneseil'

: ek druk jou dun middel styf in my in
gly my hande met die sweet langs jou gladde bergrug op
druk oor jou nek met my hande en voel
die angs in die liefdesknoop oor my loop
soos heuning oor 'n metaalblad
wat skreeu om sensueel ritmies gespeel
gevorm te word

jou hande lê oor my nek oor my skouers druk jy my
vas in die grond in sodat ek onder jou kan groei
beweeg jou bolyf ritmies op en af soos 'n slangdanser
'n oermooie gladde reptiel wat in my bloei

en in die maalpoel van die metaalsiel
sien ek my in jou dans
:: as jy te naby my staan
hou ek my pose maar in die donkerte
van my verbeelding kyk ek tussen die sterre
na jou haastige lyf en vol lippe
speel die groen in jou oë woud-woud met my
terwyl ek my hande van jou nie meer kan afhou nie
en my mond van joune nie meer kan wegskeur nie

\\verloor jouself in my, donker man
selfs met jou skild aan, terwyl die koue om die ruite wasem
jy my inasem   \\verloor jouself in my wentelbaan
heg jou wysheid aan my maan
speel met verf in jou hande aan my lyf
en maak my 'n bloeisel wat weer en weer bot
om die onperfekte planeet
van lank lank gelede was daar
te besweer
en ek jou vir altyd in my nuut kan agterhaal

om op 'n sagverlate klimaks te reis
sonder om 'n afskeid totsiens te soen

      met my kaal hande
hou ek die gladde metaalbeeld
met my arms gelig in 'n volmaannag
trek ek my vingerpunte oor sy skerp flitsende lyne
sonder dat die beeld sny deur my vlees
om hom op die rant te balanseer
'n juggler met vuurballe
wat Jupiter – die rooi rouende planeet –
met sy kinetiese energie
voortdurend uitdaag

'n reis getrek na die lyne in my hand

In Ronnie se Sex Shop kroegstop in die Kaap
het ek 'n naam uitgekrap
teen die toiletmure
teen die deure met 'n mes
op die mure tussen duisende ander
het ek 'n e-kaart vasgespyker
met 'n moerse swaar hamer
wat verander het in 'n swaard
: (al het 'n paar mense my snaaks aangekyk
het hulle my maar laat begaan) :

'kyk, die vrou is mal' | die mal vrou kyk
na haarself met 'n swaard omhoog
gelig in die spieël
en sien 'n naam
skuins agter haar linkeroor weerskaats
soos gesigte in die water van 'n bergstroom
in die loomheid van 'n laatmiddag
na 'n lang reis vol lyne wat kruis en dwars
dubbelsinnig gewetenloos haar greep vooruitloop
in are wat uitstaan in die blou-blou hemel
soos hande ineenverstrengel
die snare in die lyf trek
in die stroom stomend in- uit- in-
uitspoel

maar die stroom se droom moes val
skielik || die snare moes rek en uitrek
verder en verder om te raak
waar dit vroeër so spontaan
met sensuele vingers sag en sekuur
reg die lyf bespeel het
met erotiese note, eg oorspronklik
kreatief gespanne
oor eksotiese tale heen
oor die bene met vingers wat masserend
hul weg baan
na bo tussen die dye druk en los

met die hand wat ferm op die onderlyf rus
sag en harder
opreis na borste waar lippe en vel
ontmoet
hande vinniger vinniger speel
op die snare
tussen sweet en sap sappiger perske
en mango
spanspek O die smaak van die binnevrug
wat uitroep om geëet te word, UitRoep
Roep Harder
Sagter Sensueler die naam van alle name...

onverwag-s ja, êrens in die middelste lustige land van passie
voel jy jou lyf styftrek rek
strek verby 'n vallende engel se hande
al weet jy die doel van die draai van die gedig
was om die gevalle droom te benoem te beskryf
te versweer vervloek weer en weer
terwyl naby
nader soos die middelste onverwagte strofe
'n Ander in swart leer skielik oorkant jou staan
met bewende hande want hy ruik jou hare onder hom
die 'Angel' van 'n vorige lewe
wat jou geoliede lyf toevou
'n rou wouddroom
en sy hart klop wild
want in jou oë sien hy sy eie begeerte
in sy keel klop die angs
wat bevryding bring soos 'n allerheiligste voorspel
in sy hande voel hy 'n landskap
wat hom oorweldig
betowerend laat gryp na lug
voor die warmte van jou ingehoue asem
hom alle grense laat vergeet
verbreek en in sy honger hande
voortdurend verower hou

terwyl in donderstorm lig en droom
in half-donker skaars merkbare woorde
hul strewe ontketting

om saam met reën die aarde te transformeer
die name met 'n swaardslag
wat weer lig straal na die lyne van jou hand
die ritme in die lyf
in jou oopgekloofde skedel waaruit woorde peul

die dood het 'n naam geword
die naam 'n vrou
wat swaard omhoog gelig tussen woude
die pad na die vreemdste wildste land
oopkap: om dieper te aanskou, my lief
waar die oorsprong van alle sprokies lê:

kantelkop verkragter

ek het die soliede hamer van die huis af saamgesleep
hy het saam met my geklim op die vliegtuig
saam met my gekantel toe die tuig se vlerk
afsak en optrek na die hemel
saam met my die naar kol van sy verraad
op my maag voel draai

ja, dieselfde hamer wat die skroewe van 'n kuns-matige voël
van die muur bo my vuur afgekap het
een dag toe universele oë my begoël
-end dopgehou het
my geskenk aan die verlede
wat gril tot in sy diepste geveerde wese

op die berg, van ronnie se sex shop af
staan die falliese simbool met sy kop skuins gedraai
onder 'n groter as lewensgroot tepel
sien ek sy mond daarom vou
voel ek sy tong om en op my
klit o rus oral aan my lyf skuif
sleep   sluip

behaag ek my in sy vals ontdekkings
wriemelend op die bed
in queen elizabeth park in swartblou kar
buite die grot by breakfast rock
in die wit uitstalkamertjie in die TAG
agter groot uitstalborde in die DAG
in die botaniese tuine in durban
agter bome op 'n vreemde warm planeet
in 'n antieke winkel tussen antieke meubels
wat ruik na herinneringe
en in ronnie se sex shop stop
teen vuil 3-30 mure vasgedruk
in 'n see vol wilde strome. O ja
ons skree Halt. Dead Blank. Net daar.
Net hier.

die blou bakkie voor het 'n snaakse vorm

ons sny verby
dit voel soos die vliegtuig se vlerk
wat in die lug op swaai
soos ek val oor yster met 'n lewenswaar hamer
en die berg se tepel hemelgroot voor my opstaan
die hemel se blou witoop en helder skyn
en my hare rooilank in die sonlig blink
langer as wat hy ooit sal onthou
"Cutur h air-what t mean " Sent 3-Jan-2003 01:01:12
soos ek woorde oor en oor
inkrimp tot daar niks vir hom oor is nie

die voël suig met 'n slag op my houtvloer af
haak eers vir 'n oomblik vas aan my kaggelkap
val dan met die klank van metaal wat metaal klap
'n groot gat in my pragtige oregonhoutvloer
dat die planke oranjeswart oopspat

ek sien die berg se tepel het in die helfte gesplit
met die draai van die pad
want hy't met sy gesplete tong aan haar gesuig
met sy psigopaties-skisofreniese soen
haar soepel skoonheid middeldeur gesny
haar soel bestaan verloënend en verlate agtergelaat
in die gesplete hede in'n ver verlate Kaapse landskap
ver van haar tropiese bestaan

en ek skreeu
die lyflike lieflike onge
loofliikste orgasme van sy gedwonge metaalsoen uit
teen die wêreld van onbegrip wat in my wriemel
en woel soos 'n bynes in sy moer gepluk
'n deurmekaargeskopte miernes
waarin klein kreatuurtjies kriewel en soek
saam met daardie ewige stilte
in wanhoop chaoties rondkrioel
soekend na sin en ritme
orde en herstel

en die wêreld die verraaier
verkragter   slagter
skutter sien wat van sy mis daad
toneel vlug   te laat

Rooi 11

terwyl ek op my agterstoep sit en liquorice eet
gin en tonic drink
om die pienk eye hoofpyne wat steek en stoot te verban
en vloek want ek het nie geduld met common pyne nie
ook nie die peinende pyn wat verteer
die stene wat ek besweer
en 'n editor wil met my gaan lunch
maar my oë is pienk
soos 'n baba se nuutgebore boude...

terwyl ek op my agterstoep
sjampanjeborrels rol
en donker
groen gras rook
om die pynende teenwoordigheid
uit te tart
kom sit 'n rooi elf op my skouer
en huil van die lag
sodat ek verbaas my act net daar stop
en hom vra: 'Fok,
wat maak jy op my seer skouer
weet jy dan nie ek het teen 'n muur vasgeloop
'n sielsmuur wat nouer
druk en ruk aan die nate van my hart'

die elf met die rooi hoed hou eg-
ter nie op met lag nie en ek vou
my hande kamma kwaad
oor die naat oor my bors en sê hey
jy met die blosende gelaat
sonder respek vir my rooi oë
my misnoë
jy wat my skouers laat gloei
met jou lang stert oor my blaaie bloei
jy wat elf wolke om my draai
in die bewegings van my heupe rondswaai
asof ek nie kan raai...

die elf met die rooi halo vee sy trane af
beweeg sy lang vinger van bo
van die middel van my voorkop
af tot op my lippe sodat ek nie kan praat nie
hy trek my in
sy kring en plant sy onsterfbare glimlag
in die geheime in my mond

die groot val

Bagdag val onder die vyand se skeel oog
Iemand val bo van 'n trap af
Superman val vloeiend bo van die spook
NYtorings in 'n swierige draai by my gesigsveld
verby
en een of ander onsigbaar vlieënde karakter
val met 'n moerse sprong van bo die plafon
om 'n ander
in sy bed te skop dat blou bloed pers spat
in water
'n hadida val uit die lug om rasend te land
op my grasperk
waar hy wurms trek
en skree haadiedaaaaa
Michealangelo val vanuit sy blou illusie
van 'n religieuse hemel waaragter hy skuil
waar hy met sy nek te lank na bo gedraai
die Sisteense Kapel bly opereer
omdat hy een mens
in die oë nie kan kyk nie
| soos 'n engel wat nie kan praat nie
omdat 'n harige gog hom
in sy keel gebyt het |

// die onengel Val \\
van hoër as die Sisteense Kapel
ondertoe
die groot Val van die verloënaar
wat sy kop oopkloof :: op die sementblad
onder sy agterdeur ver onder die woud
die wond gaan haal wat hy jare gelede begin maak het

:: op die sypaadjie ver van die huis af val
en val en val hy in sy genadelose onkunde in
in die steenkoolwerf waar die swart roet
van die spoor oor die lyne van sy gesig loop
soos rioolpype in die on van niks raaksien
van niks weet niks en niemand mag sien nie

#ek weet ek oortree oor die sintuie heen#
vat kortpaaie om die verdriet
op die grootpad mis te loop
hardloop steeds alleen in onderpapagaaiberg
in kronkelpaadjies rond
terwyl die grootpad my in sypaadjies onderdompel
in rioolwater smyt
om my met al die seëninge van die verlede te doop
tot ek verdrink in weemoed
en die terughouding op my val
'n swaarder las as wat ek gekies het om te dra

hansel and gretel

hansel and gretel w-rite a fairy tale
in a red room
on a mattress in front of a blind
cutting the sun's warmth through their bodies

hansel and gretel look into each other
see a spaceship knock its propeller into the ceiling
lift off into the galaxy

hansel and gretel hear the trance sounds
of their flight in the universe
vibrate   see halos around stars
feel their bodies blend in ecstasy
until they meet   in the sky

hansel and gretel laugh
cut words into their tale
play a game
no one can imitate

hansel and gretel discover the
'origin-all'
in that cardinal room
beneath a full moon
naked   painting stripes

silent seduction

> *You have killed the child in me. Never again will you feel her*
> *sunlight on your skin or touch her golden hair. Never see the*
> *forest in her eyes and taste her honey.*
>
> *To the extent that knowledge takes itself for an end*
> *it founders upon the blind spot.*
> **George Bataille**

Baitse Mokiti

That's Me

That's me in the mirror
bald-eyed ugly
fungi-boned creature
short as a stick
calypso worn dungarees
sheering my thoughts
trimming tendrils from words
stolen from china microphones
and fishing

for compliments
I read the personals
wearing nothing but ginat saucers
spelling my name like A_B_C
as mandatory when
spreading yourself thin
mincing my paper
I chew on stature:
"Young vibrant, fun girl
25-30, ready for possibilities"
and I look possible
if entering from the right

Morning

Morning finds her on a boulder
Tightly wrapped in surrender,
The wind having grown old
There's no forever today.

Way above gathering clouds
There's a sky travelling still,
Moving out of his lips
Troubling words find their peace.

When morning returns
It is with thoughts of new days,
Swept beaches smaller seas
This is goodbye to old pain.

The boys in my life

I like the boys who walk me home
Carrying me back to keep me safe
All the way plotting a romance
Ignoring the signs with abundance;

I like the boys whose arms meet mine
With perfect knots lovers' hearts
And all the weighing me up
Looking past the jeering eyes;

I like the lies the boys preach
Of marriage to me they speak
That type of love should be a prize
Or feverish joy if it is to last;

I like the glow my boys wear
My common smile Jezebel's ghost
Standing aloof from bleeding-heart stares
I catch teardrops in eyes that are bare;

I like the songs the boys sing
Urgent looks like boomerangs
I know well when they come back
With no aces in their decks;

What I don't like on the other hand,
Are the boys who ignore me.

Daifern

Shallow graves are being emptied
The coming rains in waiting
Water needs to birth anew
All earth that has since died
The fallen nature of our being
Carries danger sown in fear
Resting in pleas are our deeds
This is where we stand
Hiding no peace.

The slaughter of the innocents

Early morning came early
Moving sunshine's all-yellow
My bloated belly all around
My joyful soul losing sound

I was netting yet still
Darling dreams for the morrow
When a slap like a bat's
Chased my dreams to sorrow

Symphonic night breezes dead
My faith in healing was dismissed
There they were, the feet
Goose-stepping over all the squares

No uncertainty to be seen
Even if all the innocents were to scream
So I cried when I had tears
No good mornings to be had

But I saw his rueful glee
Pouring well the brewing tea.

Someday

I will read them to myself
All the words I couldn't write,
With the music thrown down
I'll have silence for my foe
With this space for my undoing
All the truth will come out.

And I shall hate every moment
Carrying back fallen dreams,
With my future not quite settled
I will bring all my cursing
With my mind all broken
Just my mouth will lie open.

Growing tired

The love doesn't fall
Where it normally should,
The heart has grown tired
Watching the beggars
Carrying their plight,
The man is not my darling
Though the speech is one of desiring,
I grow wearier grow even more tired
Watching the windows
With all of the missing pictures
The hideous wall
Balancing all to a fault
The repetitive words
The nothing-here-but-echoes,
I cut away all his words
Growing tired growing dimmer,
And blow out the dying candles
Having nothing more to whisper.

For my other

For my other I will desire,
Marrying good with
Sunday roasts toasting,
The never planning
Of early morning glories,
Lighting in cigarettes
The loving after the sighing;
Fiery bacon summery aching,
Coffee-musing days not
Barley-lapping brays,
Sweet nothings in our ears
Gentle dabs on derrieres,
Freshly picking thoughts
Orange juice and sprightly walks.

Unwritten

Staring at my words
I feel
The fear of moving
Peel back
White on white, so stark
The little clean
I feel,

No more afraid
I twitch
Dowsing fingers, I page
Shelling cobwebs
I write
All of my truth
You'll know,

Leftover feelings
Are spared
Lost in a letter
My breast,
Bleeding no ink, unwritten
Safe in my hands
Unknown.

Writer's block – blank thoughts on lined paper – 22.5cm x 16.5cm

11.5cm favourite pen
On flat board
Blue plastic cap
Nib northwest diagonal
Framed in 22.5cm x16.5cm
Rectangular plain paper
Crossing 31 blue gaps
0.5cm widely spaced
Severe red margin
1.5cm to the left
Starting never ending
Inspiration: empty wording.

Myesha Jenkins

The Nature of Me

I am nice,
when I should spit
I understand
as much as I hurt
I give
when my palms are fists
I am open
though the void is endless
I listen
and speak back my truth.

I stand.

Autobiography

It was too early
Blood, blood, everywhere
mother hemorrhaging, the priest gave her last rites
sorry father, no hope for baby
Nineteen forty-eight
I was born a rebel at birth.

I grew, played rough, was smart, had friends
sprouted hair, grew tits and started bleeding
By eight I knew my body was
fearful, shameful, dangerous
That year my brother got married
I was raised like an only child.

I grew into a tomboy girl, achieving girl, woman girl
My first political march at 14 for four black girls just like me
blown up in a Birmingham church.

I loved, married, divorced, lived on stages pretending to be whatever
you needed me to be and I drank
College, Black Power, sexuality, a new name,
given two months "in Africa" and I drank
Became a communist, studied Marxism Leninism,
thought I was a revolutionary
went to meetings, led marches, learned to shoot, organized events,
went to Cuba, to Nicaragua and I drank
Women's Day, AGMs, demonstrations, speaking tours, pamphlets,
summations, fundraisers and I drank
Jesse Jackson campaign, Black Community Task Force, Women's Building,
Bay Area Anti-Apartheid Network, Venceremos Brigade, Somos Hermanas
and I drank
LA, DC, San Francisco, Atlanta, Berkeley, Oakland and I drank
Bill, Fred, James, Tony, Leon, Ralph, Andy, Vicki, Joy, Michelle, Sandi.

And I drank into insanity
denial, secrets, convulsions, hopelessness
weed, pills, cocaine
Couldn't be there in my skin
At the bottom there was only up.

Born again at 38
The goodness of life
began in my struggle to stay sober
to change my outlook on life
I have survived earthquakes, fires, floods and tornados
nearly drowned in Hawaii
Touched an ancient religion
Met revolutionaries.

I left that home at 44 and made a new one
South Africa's spirit of freedom absorbed me
I found a poet's voice, enjoy young lovers, shout in jazz clubs
and cry for beauty.

There are things that I'm not proud of –
abortions, infidelity, rage, dogmatism, adultery, violence
but I have come to accept what I am.

Worked for rich people and poor people
mostly to change the circumstances of women and black people
Sadly never had children.

Still other memories –
tree-lined beaches, abandoned cars with names, road trips, hot tubs,
the friendship of women.

I remain a sucker for a jazz musician or poet
Conscious of politics but no longer active
Obatala and the ancestors light my path
Discovered flying
I find much to be happy about.

Mother

My mother speaks a foreign language
it is only in the past tense
struggling to explain the times
when she was loved
and in control of her world
forcing me to remember
things and events
that are now only important
to her

I have lost the skill of
building pedestals for the dead
counting the scars left from cancerous intrusions
and storing papers and rubberbands

Long forgotten is the wedding dress in your closet
like the love you taught me to want
The pleasantries of the lady you raised me to be
all gag in my throat

I only mourn the little girl
never smiling in your picture books
unknown in the wilderness
without maternal arms

My mother speaks a foreign language
she can't hear my voice
although my tongue moves swiftly
in and out of this life
I've built for myself

I am a woman now
speaking in tongues of the present
calling from a whirlwind of swirling life
listening to strange truths
playing with the energies of a universe
flying out into the future

My mother's tongue is in the past
I don't know how to speak it anymore.

Anticipation

In the vulnerable hills where my hope is fed
the many tribes of me are listening for you

Camped around fires in the valleys waiting to hear your song
Those at the river have already started drumming
Children have put on their brightest colours
Dancers in the lowlands have been practicing for weeks
Holy men gather under moonlight gleaming in ash and clay

We are listening for you
We are listening for you

The Launch

I saw you there
with all your past
draped like jewellery
on your arms

adorned and shimmering
with painted baubles, fools' gold
cheap pearls, false smiles
traditional beads at your waist

I saw you there
weighed down with promises
of redemption and glory
glinting off the chandeliers

You must have liked
glittery things once
must have required
those flashy accessories
tormented by your ashen nakedness

Strange how I
have discovered
the natural beauty of
silk and feathers, cotton and wool
the warm glow of my own
Light

Heritage

My people were warriors
I am a feminist
My people told stories
I write poems
My people worked the land
I work in concrete office blocks
My people were healers
I listen to hurts
My people raised families
I grow flowers
My people built houses
I build communities
My people were survivors
I am a fighter
My people crossed a nation
I cross oceans
My people were dreamers
I believe in God
My people lived in big gulps
I listen for the sun to set
My people were African, Choctaw, Irish and Cherokee
I am black

Jazz Music

Lift me, lift me
Let it be said
Let it be done

Genius black angel brother

Take me in your power
Fly me to green
Rest me on your cool silk pillow
Tease me with your conga tongue

Lift me, lift me
Genius black angel brother

Piano singing
a beauty place
in trills and shimmers
my secret place

Tenor reaching
out of the universe
into my pain
Yes, play my note

Pulling on that bass
your fingers just won't stop
playing with my mind

Spirit breath
spits like ember sparks
shooting in the wind

My body mimics
your rhythm kisses
till reality shifts

Staggered
Incoherent

Paralysed
by your vision

Genius black angel brother
Lift me, lift me
Let it be said
Let it be done

Lift me
Lift me

Kids

1. Self-Definition

Kids in sunglasses
little girls with purses
in costume
superman
batman
ballerinas
spiderman
fairy queens

You see them in the supermarket
on the way to pre-school
attached to mom busily shopping
fashion conscious visionaries
imitating their heroes and heroines

They want to move
to fly
to show their special powers

They know who they are
and refuse to stay in the box
we call childhood
no matter what

2. Freedom Fighters

You can see their eyes
that two year old
on soft chubby legs
the three year old
darting from a careless hand

Amok in open spaces
they run into
the bigness of the world

train stations
airports
bus depots
hotel lobbies
force them to break those chains
and run to freedom

Makwapeni

I see us in the picture
posing so casually,
like we didn't know.
Your big hand draping over my shoulder
almost touched my breast.
Leaning my hip into yours
I held tight to your waist.
A surprisingly comfortable fit
me nestled close, safe
under your arm.

Animal

that was hiding
comes awake
lives in me
driving
pulsing
sweating
feeling my body
frantic
and nothing else
desperate in its
desire to have you
deeper
harder
grabbing it
wet
pulling it
all over me
inside out of me
pushing it
looking in your eyes
when we opened up
it came out
and we both survived
toe to toe
and liked it

Creatures of the night

Unknown and uninvited
they didn't like the meat
they said it didn't have salt.
But they partied under the trees til dawn
singing to Donny Hathaway and Ma Brrr
drinking brandy and smoking spliff
even went out for more beer
dancing
til the light sent them indoors.

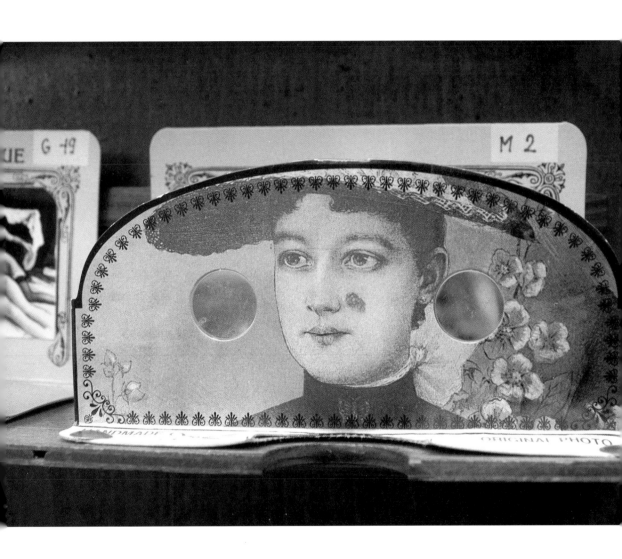

Arja Salafranca

.... Still you go through the motions:
eat at restaurants, make more conversations
with strangers than you do with friends.
At some point you will sound cynical, and that is part of it.
It's to be expected, and no-one will wonder
why you feel that way.

Birth, death, divorce, marriage, dating, dying,
closing a business deal.

You slot your note into the machine, waiting for the tinkle of change
to emerge − less than what you put in ....

We reach out

We reach out,
and touch air.
Blindly we grope,
dig fingernails in beach sand,
gritty particles under our fingers.
We scrabble, eyes closed
against the midday sun,
irritated, as the last sandal
eludes our grasp.
We are distracted;
the husbands appear,
trailing children,
a water bucket, a spade,
as the salty tang of seawater
clings to their hair.
Idly, our toes reach down,
grope for the last sandal,
red nailpolish glinting against the sandy beach.
There are whole lives
that have gone missing.
The magazine we have been reading
slides onto the sand.
A woman laughs out of a photograph,
lips lush and ripe.
We reach out again,
feel the strap of the missing sandal.
A child sees an ice-cream vendor, wants a sucker.
We watch as the child licks the
green ice, pink tongue taking on a
fake greenish stain.
We wriggle our toes in the sand,
feeling for the sandal.
All that is available to us, right now,
is a stretch of beach,
a roiling ocean and white picturesque waves,
beach houses ascending the hill,
the midday sun,
the child sucking green ice,

the husband's head full of sand,
and the sandal burrowing deeper
into the sand as we frantically
search for it, burying it
even deeper as we try to find it.
We reach out,
and touch air.
Other lives are intangible.
Unable to step out of the frame
of our chosen reality,
we reach out and touch air.
The sun pierces the back of our heads,
and we search for a sandal,
watch the blinding light of midday
burn the waves silver.

A woman selecting cleaning fluids

In the aisle of a supermarket,
I see the denim dress splayed over
the pregnant stomach.
I watch the easy nonchalance of a woman
selecting cleaning fluids.
Sashaying down the aisle
she looks at me, is about to
turn away when there's an moment of recognition.
I too have remembered her,
and I avert my eyes,
I won't acknowledge her.
She realises this and looks away.

I knew her
long ago, at high school.
She knows things about me then.
I'm not proud of the person I was,
or of the things I didn't manage to do.
So in that instant, I choose
as I hadn't once been able.

I choose to ignore this happy, pregnant
woman with the unchanged features of a young girl.
I choose to stride on, to cut her off,
to deny her the chance to see
what I've done.

Another day

Another Sunday, another sunset.
Another flick of the indicator as the sun
bathes the veld in peach hues.
Another drumming of the engine
as years seem to pass.

Is this what they mean by getting older?
Scattered across the table like wedding confetti,
breathing in someone else's smoke,
watching a man drink coke in a glass full of ice,
you drive home,
hand in a bag of coconut ice,
mind wandering over yellow-tipped roofs.
Another highway cuts the highway,
you stop,
wait for lights to change.
Music dies as the engine revs.

What do they mean?
They mean it's nearly six o'clock
on a Sunday afternoon, and you are driving alone.
They mean that time leaps on, and they mean that
you'll continue to have lunch or dinner with strange men.
It may take a while yet.
They mean no harm as they pound you with
questions, expectations, accusations.

Still you go through the motions:
eat at restaurants, make more conversations
with strangers than you do with friends.
At some point you will sound cynical, and that is part of it.
It's to be expected, and no-one will wonder
why you feel that way.

Birth, death, divorce, marriage, dating, dying,
closing a business deal.

You slot your note into the machine, waiting for the tinkle of change
to emerge – less than what you put in.

Kissing the wall

The woman's face is unadorned,
slightly wrinkled. Her head is
covered in a pink and white scarf.
Zooming in, the camera watches the slightly pursed lips,
as oblivious to the world,
she tenderly inclines her head, eyes closed,
and, in an act of faith, kisses the wall.
In that instant she releases her longing
and the pain, the wall
a forgiving, deserving lover.
You can't see her body,
only her passion as she leans in,
oblivious, lost
in the seal of her kiss.

Foreign ice

Frost covers the grass, the trees, the shed,
the benches in the garden.
It looks like snow.
The pavements are icy.
I crunch along, leaving footprints.
The ice melts slowly, but appears again by morning.
The sky is almost cloudless,
aeroplanes take off, trailing two
white streams as they ascend;
these curve across the sky and fade.

My boots are ten years old.
A decade ago they also walked London's streets.
But it was different then –
didn't seem so blue and sunny;
but I was warmer then –
a student in love with being a foreigner,
seeing it for the first time,
and nightmares came only at night.

This time I choke on English bread,
can't find the foods I am used to.
This time I tread resentfully,
wanting to make my flat vowels
stand out among clipped ones.
This time the weather is cold,
a bright, brittle cold.
This time I have to live here.

Exile's icy. You will never be English.
You will never be a Londoner
rushing along the pavements at
breakneck speed to catch a train.
You will never share memories of frozen childhoods
with people who spent winters wrapped in parkas,
hands wrapped around mugs of sweet tea.
You don't know about making snowmen,
or days when school was cancelled because of raging snowstorms.

Instead you listen incredulously to a woman on TV
complain there aren't enough types of contraceptives available.
Now you come from a place where contraception is not always a given,
where bread and butter is exactly that: a meal, something to avoid starving.
What's a TV debate among sophisticates who've never been hungry,
and want a supermarket of contraceptives!

The ironies lie there in the crunch of boots.
The jarring clash of haves and have-nots
slam up against my amazement at the complaints
when trains are late (aren't they grateful they come at all?),
or that the national health system is in tatters
(aren't they glad to have one?).

In Harrow the shopping district
has been closed off to traffic
and cinnamon pancake smells fill the air.
Familiar shops cluster along paved walkways:
Marks and Spencers, Next, New Look, Barclays Bank.
We huddle in our jackets
at one with the crowd of shoppers,
people on leave, buying Christmas presents.
At one and yet so separate from these shoppers
with their jobs and accents,
shared memories of English winters.
We stare from the outside,
spending pounds, handling the Queen's face.

Harrow becomes a part of us.
I'll remember it months later,
recreate it in dreams.
So quickly that transition from winter
to summer, only a flight away.
I'll never be a Londoner,
I realise this as a bus takes us down
an unfamiliar street
on a cold English day.

On the trains

There were women with bulging bellies
who chose to wear skin tight tops
showing their opulent flesh and pale pink stretch marks.
There were women who concluded business deals
on cellphones as they travelled home to supper after eight.
There were businessmen in suits with tired eyes,
and old men who held onto walking sticks.
There were young men who rocked to music
from tiny earphones slotted into their ears,
the music so loud you heard the tinny jagged sounds
over the train wheels. Once an old man shouted:
"You'll be deaf by the time you're thirty!" as he shuffled off.

One night, slightly later than the rest,
a couple boarded the train.
The woman was not pretty, her eyes tired and defeated.
The man's domed forehead glistening,
his hard bulky body splayed out on the seat.
They argued. She tried to be quiet,
whispering disagreements.
But he bellowed and swore,
"How the hell should I know?"
"I drive a car, I don't take the train."
I saw her embarrassment, she looked quickly at me,
as I witnessed the fight,
her unhappiness, his boorishness.
I tried not to look, not to deepen her shame.
But we kept hearing his voice,
his foot banging on the floor.
And as we got off, I imagined
her unhappiness continuing
like the train straight into darkness.

The elephant is unhappy

The ground is squelchy underfoot.
The elephant is unhappy.
The grass sparse, wet.
A dog is chained to a table.
"I am on guard," is the sign on a caravan.
At the next, a woman holding a cigarette
retreats to its shuttered interior.
The chained dog finds shelter beneath the camping table,
tail between its legs.

In the field by the main road
the elephants have attracted onlookers.
A mother holds her child.
The elephants are still, silent.
An elephant blows dust onto herself,
burrowing a hole into the ground as she sucks up dust,
blows it, uses her trunk to enlarge a hole at her feet.
Her hide is wrinkled grey.
Beyond her, cars stream along the wide,
sun-bleached road.
Men sort hay and grass.

Tethered by foot, held by a stake in the ground,
she moves, her ears flap, her trunk grasps the air;
she sways, the chain stretches,
and just before she reaches the end of it's pull,
she stops, sways, knowing she can't go any further.
Her trunk reaches out again,
her big body trembling slightly,
a foot moves forward. The elephant is unhappy.

Silently, we walk away. The ground is
squelchy underfoot, and the caravans
are inscrutable: you can't see through
their small lace-covered windows.

The monk meditates

The monk meditates,
waits, eyes downcast.
He is small beside the huge,
benevolent Buddha.
The altar is littered with offerings and
portions of rice.
The monk waits,
closed in on himself,
orange robes sweaty.
He does not notice the camera
or the sun hitting the statue;
he does not see the streak
of the flash as he sits.

A young monk,
he watches, in his mind,
the departing images of his
mother and brothers –
they had walked away into the
mist that day.
The monk has been offered
up to someone else's dreams.
He sits obediently waiting.
The worshippers crowd in,
bringing flowers, more offerings;
praying, bartering for better lives.

The monk sits,
expressionless, empty.
He has just seen a vision of
what will be.
He remains seated,
eyes downcast, hands sheltering his belly
while the Buddha looks on.

II

In the distance
the mother and her children reach their home.
She stares at the darkened purple mountains,
the trail they have walked.
The monastery is far away, hidden.
The trail crumbles in the wind.
The children are hungry:
she gets the fire going, puts food and
water in a pot. Her husband calls.
As the shadows lengthen
night eats the earth,
silence squeezes the village,
smoke drifts away.
Fires smoulder, re-ignite,
animals call in the distance,
children snore lightly,
a sweaty, salty odour mixes with the air.
The pot, big and blackened,
swings slightly over the ash-filled pit.
The mother makes out shapes in the
ink-black darkness, her rough hands tired as
she tries to remember what has been forgotten.

Makhosazana Xaba

Waking up

In the early morning of my life
I did not hear the cocks crowing
I did not wake up as with my peers.

In the mid morning of my life
I watched the shadows move
Without much thought, I followed.

In the midday of my life
I felt the scorching heat of the sun
burn through my hair, right into my brain
I knew then that I wouldn't let the sun burn me
ever again.
I didn't go in the sun at midday again.

In the afternoon of my life
as I watch the sun set,
you rise ever so slowly behind its rays
to be my sun in the night
lighting my consciousness as I sleep
I dream, dream, dream you.
Slowly, I wake up to
you being in my life,
turning it around
moulding, it in ways I never imagined.

You, the first woman I love
in the afternoon of my life.

Farting knees 1: talking to myself

When I vomit,
it will be through my forehead,
because my ears oscillate,
my eyes bounce in and out of their sockets,
my lips pound,
my neck wobbles,
my ribs grind over my spine,
my nipples engrave your name
on my abdominal wall,
the wall that's slowly freezing
from the shock
of watching my body's contents
metamorphose into thick gelatine,
forming a slippery veneer on the ground.

My once-rounded ass
is scattering
like shattered glass,
bit by piece.

My thighs are concrete poles
as my knees fart unstoppably
in this vortex of indescribable emotions
caused by your persistent indecision.

My arms, amputated,
roll alongside my torso,
careful not to pick up the slime
from the now-unsteady ground.

I'm resigned to farting knees,
my lower legs are phantoms.

Views of my Cancerian friends

Camilla Abrahams, my friend,
says she hates Coloureds:
"Girlfriend, I won't even go to their house parties.
Man, these people, they all live in Pretoria,
they say they won't even set foot in Jo'burg.
They ask me do you still live in Yeoville?"

Camilla, a single parent through divorce,
Cape Coloured to the core,
says she hates Coloureds for their narrow-mindedness.
That's why she chills out at Time Square
where her Cape Colouredness doesn't make her square.
Born in July, she holds her heart with warmth.

Fatima Moodley, my friend,
says she hates Indians.
"Khosi, I don't want them in my salon.
These people, you have no idea how racist they are.
They all hate Africans.
They say I'm crazy to be friends with them.
They say I should move out of Yeoville.
They ask me, 'Why do you do their hair?'"

Fatima, a single parent through divorce,
Indian to the core, from the cane fields of Natal,
runs her own hair salon a few blocks away from me.
Born in July, she listens over heads, lets relief live.

Mantombi Mthiyane, my friend,
says she hates Jo'burg.
"Man, I don't know how you live in this city
Too fast, too big, too inhuman, too…
Everyone tells me your area is dangerous.
How come you feel safe?
Is it safe for your daughter?
They tell me all the *makwerekwere*
choose to live in your area."

Mantombi, a single parent through divorce,
born and bred in Upington,
says she hates Jo'burg's pace
'cause it would not give her time to dress in lace.
Born in July, she's as regal as a queen.

Trivia holds

Your armpits stare at me as you
knot your hands firmly behind your head.

They invite my fingertips for a walk,
maybe a game to count your pores –
tickling you till you start to giggle,
then laugh; laugh till you cry,
cry till your hair grows back again.

Your hair, now back to its black and white,
beckons my palms,
asking them for stroking –
maybe backwards and forwards stroking
till you begin to slumber then dream,
dream till it's changed back
to the red of abandon.

Your nipples give a bulge of tenderness
through your light blue top.
They speak the language of magicians.
I see them rise, your breasts filling up.
I see your breasts placing themselves,
in sheer abundance, in the space between your bent arms
while we all watch, motionless.

Your face forlorn, you speak again: "Trivia spoils."
But, trivia also holds,
holds like a vessel.
It contains like the horizon.
It pierces through air tight membranes
delivering release, then ultimate freedom.
It's as real, as worthy, as air particles.

Mornings on weekdays

Pronutro for baby brother.
Sour porridge for the rest of us,
For ma and pa, sweet milky coffee, as well.
For our own health, no coffee allowed, we were
too young for coffee, too old for milk and pronutro.
The kitchen in motion, eight watchful eyes on ma.
Our skilful hands, hover over baby's bowl.

Some days brought luck for one or two,
a spoon or two from brother's bowl.
The rules were clear, ours to follow:
finish the porridge or no bread will follow.

Pronutro sometimes sweet and milky,
our porridge lumpy on days.
The kitchen in motion, eight vigilant eyes fixed on ma.
Our masterful limbs carry us to the garden
to bury the sour remains,
then scurry us back to the kitchen
for that well earned slice of bread.

Some days brought luck for one or two,
roaming chickens didn't dig up the sour remains.

Wishing

To my right, a wine glass and a heater.
To my left, a peeled naartjie on a saucer.
Between my legs, a packet of macademia nuts.
In front, a television screen.
It's a Saturday afternoon, a freezing June day,
And I'm watching *Imizwilili*, a program of choral music.
I watch the Drakensburg Boy's Choir,
And I begin to wish.

These boys, they sing in many languages.
These boys, they sing in ways
I've never heard boys sing before.
Then they move, clap hands.
Then they turn around, as they sing.
It's a cold June, I'm seeing boys
whose voices warm my room, then my heart
and I continue to wish.

They do the soprano, the alto, the tenor.
Tuning fork in his right hand,
Their conductor's face moves with them.
His grey head and aging body pulls them to him.
Their eyes find a home on his face.
But at the same time their voices envelop my body.
I sit there and watch, then join them in song
and my wish turns into music.

The woman on the piano's
Eyes and fingers dance on the keys,
The boys take turns at the microphone.
Each one, just himself.
Each one, at one with the rest –
Black, white, soprano, alto, tenor.
Various drums beat to the boys' voices.
I sit there and watch, then I see my father
and my wish becomes a body.

To my right, a wine glass and a heater.
To my left, a naartjie on a saucer.
Between my legs, a packet of macademia nuts.
In front, a television screen.
It's a Saturday afternoon, freezing June day.
The Drakensburg Boys Choir on the programme *Imizwilili*
Make me wish my father was my son.

Locked

They sit in the kitchen
a small mosaic table between them.
Two blue serviettes,
two silver forks, two plates,
hot chicken curry, untouched.

Four eyes locked, silent tears.
The wall clock turns on itself.
Thunder.
From the dark outside, now and again,
lightning.

Skin Speak

The dead speak.

The dead speak to us.
They put words on our tongues,
insert lines, add choruses.

They package their spirits
in invisible wireless tubes that link to our ears.
They parcel their thoughts
in thick blinking doses that reach us in sleep.
Breathe through the pores of your skin
and the dead will speak to you, directly.

Find me a fan

Find me a fan the colour of peace.
Sit beside me fan in hand
and gently blow my face front to back,
then side to side.
Move to the space between my breasts –
it gets hotter than my face sometimes –
blow into it, over and over again.

Hopefully I will close my eyes,
and drift, begin the journey.
I will not tell you to stop.
I trust you to notice
when my face becomes
the colour of peace.

My book

My book has never been too tired to go to bed with me.
It never has a headache or needs downtime to discuss the day.
It never says: please not now, I'm not in the mood.
In fact, my book seduces me with its spine
that beckons from the shelf, yearning for my touch.
When I reach out to hold it between my fingers
it eases into them, slides into my palm, yields to my gaze.
With tenderness it lays its pages bare for me
and speaks words that carry me through waves of emotions.
When my eyes won't open and I am spent,
it rests right next to me, ready for the next round.

This dance

When did you choreograph this dance,
the dance you do so well?
This dance of yes, no   no,yes   no-yes-no,
Maybe now, maybe later,   maybeneverever, perhaps.
I watch you dance
and get an instant squint.

How did you choreograph this dance,
the dance you do so well?
This dance of yes, no   no, yes   no-yes-no,
Maybe now, maybe later,   maybeneverever, perhaps.
I watch you dance
and think your feet must hurt.

Now let me tell you something:
you will never find suitable music
for this dance you now do so well.
Rehearse in my presence if you will but
you will never perform it on stage,
no audience will pay to see it.

Why did you choreograph this dance,
the dance you do so well?
This dance of yes, no   no, yes   no-yes-no,
Maybe now, maybe later,   maybeneverever, perhaps.
I watch you dance
and wish you miss a step.

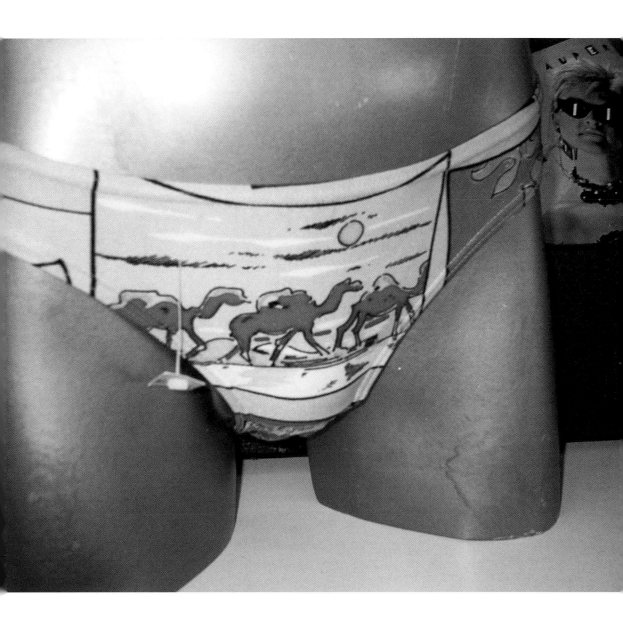

177

Riana Wiechers

.... en als wat ek is
sit vas in my kop
Europa terg vir Asië
in Afrikaste dop

en ek raak die kleur
van 'n tollende bol
'n kantel-as
sit my borskas vol ....

first resolution

first resolution
then revolution

but how can I overthrow
i f y o u k e e p r e j e c t i n g

Back then it was easy, hey
a head so soft at sixteen

to say Open Sesame
to a drunk child

+ leave her to struggle

w i l l s e e i f s h e s w i m s o r s i n k s

Because you still run away
just show me your back

see sore for mad

see asking
for missiles

Back then it was easy

hey

. . . easy when you're horny and young

these days you run
look past so quickly

see sore for mad

see mad

f o r m e

Vrydagaand 6:47 pm

die maan 'n halwe slaappil

die nag so jonk en blou

die strate ryp en besig

die berg

'n soen

vir jou

Dis oukei

Laas sondag het ek drie plate gekoop
Kosgemaak
Gedrink
Gerook

Geluister toe The Wall
+ bob dylan spin

plat herhinnering
rond + bros

(of course het twee gespring)

+ jy steeds weg
uit die ons
in die my

maar moenie 2x dink nie

moenie 2x dink nie
moenie 2x dink nie

dis ok

Mr fearful

Mr fearful
cannot tell the world
so scream to those standing closest

Mr fearful

so afraid
to be alone

to keep quiet
or
to see what's going on

fear fear Fear

makes me so fucking mad

sucks me Up

Mr fearful: the World outside

World: Mr fearful's shell

kyk baby

kyk baby
ek weet
dis 'n fokop

m a a r   j y   w e e t   h o e   d e l i c i o u s
'n   gemors   k a n   w e e s

       luister
       ek weet
       dis complicated

 maar hulle sê god is in die details   . . .

     + hoekom nie ook in ons s'n nie

     hoekom de hel nie vir ons nie

     Wat maak ons minder heilig
      as mense vir wie dit maklik was

+ wat weet jy

  anyway

van niksmagweet
     van malwagsweet

die here weet
ek bid jy weet

  e k   k a n   n i e   m e e r   a l l e e n   h i e r a a n   e et   n ie

hart tot maag

ek wonder hoe jou lyf lyk

soveel jaar al
dink ek daaraan

deesdae dink ek
so baie daaraan

wens ek kon kerslig   oor   jou   gooi

voel-voel bekyk
al jou hoeke
+ kante

van k e n tot skouers
van hart tot maag

Miskien my hand
onder laken laat glip

hoe lyk jou hande nou weer?

Wed dis lank + maer
sterk + seer

toemaar

m y   m a a g   s ê   h u l l e m o e t   m o o i w e e s

soos jy
soos Jy

van   hart

tot   maag

tonight I will

tonight I will
have to bake a tongue

with the sun's appearance
the words have to disappear

+ fist it
f i s t   i t

something over
finished

now you know
Now You Know

the truth
about me:

beast
animal

u n a b l e

beast
monster

beakframed

unoriginal
animal

dumb+angry

lonely crocodile
in word

+deed

klein drakies

hallo hallo
weer ek aan jou

met woorde vet van wind

waai blou en koud
waai weg die woede
daai waansin waar 'n sin in was
en kaarthuisgedagtes van rooi en goud

want hier's sandkasteellandkaarte
en seegras
en skulpe en dolfyne en vuur

as 'n dink mag bly staan
op 'n aand onbeskaam
– op 'n klip vol wolke
soos tafelberg vanaand –

kan ek vir altyd by jou bly

sprokies ontgin
dalk vir jou die waarheid voer

en klein-klein drakies verjaag

look at me

look at me
it's all that stays

all that stays
after all that-

All that r o c k + r o l l
all that party

all that all night

all that Naai

Do you know what déjà vu
it's crazy
I know

but it's true

all is testimony
all story

A l l   f o r   w o r d

i n   a   s o r t o f b e i n g l o s t

siamese seisoene

so siamees soos ons kon wees
die een net soos die ander
so jonk so gou so diep so braaf

ek Simpel

jy Koljander

so siamees soos ons wou wees
so hard het ek probeer
en jy, jy met die gaaptandskêr
jy byt ons middeldeur

so siamees soos net ons was
so vasgewoel in jare

en al daai blink en nat seisoene

nou net as en blare

dans (soos ek nou)

Die hartseerste dans
Was die een op die trappies
Met veertien gewere
en 'n winterstrand

die hartseerste dans
was die een deur die deure
met twee klarinette
en 'n bos wat brand

die hartseerste kans
was die waarmee jy weg is
met die sout en die sag
soos jy wou

die hartseerste dans
is die een soos alleengeit
met die sout en die sag
soos ek nou

Valium and fireballs

Valium and fireballs
work the best

the best
after 2
in the morning

o f   c o u r s e

what happened prior to
and the whole following

. . .

anyway

all that matters is

valium makes me dream of you

+ fireballs
          hurt only softly

so Valiums

+ fireballs

is the only thing to take

-pay no attention to a meal
-only after 2 in the morning

for anyone

alone

wat's 'n afrikaner

wat's 'n afrikaner?
wat's 'n kontinent?

al wat ek weet
is wat ek nie is nie

al wat ek weet
is wat ek represent

afrikaner-hater
sell-out
wigger
wannabe

boervrou
prinses
afrikanernooientjie

als behalwe
just me

en als wat ek is
sit vas in my kop
Europa terg vir Asië
in Afrikaste dop

en ek raak die kleur
van 'n tollende bol
'n kantel-as
sit my borskas vol

So wat's 'n afrikaner?
wat's 'n kontinent?

al wat ek weet
is wat ek nie is nie

al wat ek weet
is wat ek represent

Bongekile Mbanjwa

.... Lingishonele mina kababa,
Ngisho izinyembei zigeleza ezinhlathini,
Ngisho ngifulathela,
Ngifulathela ngilambatha imibuzo imi mpo.
Kanti ngingubani? ....

.... The sun has gone down on me, oh, my God!
Tears flow down my cheeks!
Even when I have turned my back,
My back turned to the world and I am empty-handed,
Questions still stand firm:
Who am I? ....

Isihluthulelo

Mina ngife olwembiza,
Mina ngife ngihamba,
Iphi imvelaphi yami?
Iphi intandokazi kazulu?
Liphi ibhodwe likazulu?

Sizobondwa ngani lesigwamba?
Sizobondelwaphi na?
Baphi bona abazosidla?
Angithi bagcwele izinkalo,
Angithi behla benyuka,
Befuna impilo yasesilungwini,
Befuna umbulalazwe.

Isizukulwane sisifumbathiseni zulu?
Isizukulwane soziqhenya ngani?
Sesi ngamaluulwane isibili,
Ngikhalela amakhehla namakhehlakazi,
Won'ayobuzwa zinyanya,
Ngebhodwe likazulu.

Ngithi mtaka mbuli uphi na?
Ngithi izwi lakho ebelingampongoloza
Sizw'isizukulwane sikazulu.
Umemezile ngaphambili ngezwa ngingadakiwe,
Ngakuzwa seliyoshona mzwakhe,
Kwezam'izindlebe.

Ho! He! Pho, uphi manje?
Zikuxhakathisile izidladla zebhubesi
Zikuxhakathise kwathulu'umoya,
Zikukinathele kwezimnyam'izisele
Ngithi zinyanya ndini niphi?
Ngithi nithule nithini amagugu eshabalala?
Sizodukuza ontwini mtakabba,
Isihluthulelo silahlekile.

Translation: Lock and key

I am a broken pot,
I am the walking dead.
Where are my origins?
Where is the favourite, KaZulu?
Where is the pot, Zulu?

With what is winter porridge going to be stirred?
Where is it going to be stirred?
Who is going to eat it?
They are wandering in the ridges,
They are walking up and down
Searching for 'western' life,
Searching for the destroyer of the land.

What are we offering to the young generation?
What will generations to come pride themselves about?
We are like bats really.
I am crying for grandmothers and grandfathers
Who will be called to account by the ancestors.

I say: where are you son of Mbuli?
I say: your voice should shout out!
Nation, grandchildren of Zulu,
You shouted in front and I was sober.
I heard you with my own ears Mzwakhe
When the sun went down.

Ho! He! Now where are you?
The lion's paws have gripped you tight.
They snapped you tight and there was silence.
They locked you inside dark cells.
I say: where are you ancestral spirits?
I say: why are you silent when our valuables disappear?
We grope in the dark, my father's child.
The key is lost.

Kungenxa Kabani

Washabalala ntomb'yomuntu
Kwabhidlik'isidleke,
Washabalala sasabalala,
Mfudumalo yekhaya uphi?
Ukhwabaniswe ngubani?

Ntombi kangqoyi,
Ushiye kuxabene ubendle,
Isisu sakho sihlukene phakathi,
Isisu sakho sibhekana ngeziqu zamehlo.
Ubundlalifa bugubuzele umqondo,

Ubundlalifa buqhoqhobele amatomu;
Ubundlalifa buxhakatisile;
Uphi uthumbu omshiye ebaleni?
Uphi umuzikayise na?
Kunjenje kungenxa kabani?

Ulele buph'ubuthongo na?
Ushiy'bambene ngezihluthu;
Ushiy'imimoya ishwilene;
Ushiy'innhliziyo zigaya izibozi;
Ushiy'isideku sibhedulkile;
Kunjenje kungenxa kabani?

Bundlalifa unecala,
Bundlalifa ungumbhidlizi,
Bundlalifa uyinswelaboya,
Ngabezezwe bengithi ungumakhi
Kanti ungumbidlizi nezinqotho zakhe.

Masami nithule nithini?
Zinyanya nithule nithini?
Kungani ukhuni luphenduke umlotha?
Ke umbuzo uyohlala umile,
Kuze kube nje, kungenxa kabani?

Translation: Whose fault is it?

You disappeared daughter,
And the nest was destroyed.
You disappeared and we scattered.
Where is the warmth of home?
Who stole you?

Daughter of Ngqoyi,
You left everything in chaos,
Your womb divided,
Your womb at loggerheads.
There is a veil across the heir's brain.

The heir is wearing bridles,
The heir has been trapped.
Where is the last child you left in the yard?
Where is the heir to the homestead?
When things are in a mess like this,
Whose fault is it?

What kind of sleep are you in?
You left the battle while hot,
You left tempers high,
You left hearts with ill-feeling,
You left the main root uprooted.

Heir, you are guilty!
Heir, you are a good-for-nothing!
Heir, you are a thief!
I thought you were a builder
But you are a real destroyer!

Mother, why are you quiet?
Ancestral spirits, why are you silent?
Why is the stick turned to ash?
The question still stands:
Things are like this,
Whose fault is it?

Uzozo

Nhliziyo uvuz'igazi,
Nhlanhl'ushabalele,
Nhlungu zomphefumulo' udlangile,
Inhlw'igcwel'intukuthelo,
Inhlw'iphuphuma inzondo,
Umcibisholo uhlaba uphindelela.

Kuza unonya,
Kufa untinyelisa okodonsi,
Kufa ugole ukhalangani,
Kufa ugole uzondeni,
Kufa ugole izimfihlo,
Wangembesa ngeminjunju.
Ngisawadla anhlamvana,
Inhliziyo yami iyolokhu ishilo ithi ndo, ndo, ndo.

Izinduduma ziphuhlile ezaleni,
Izinduduma zishwabadele iva lokungibangula,
Izindunduma zigubuzele izimpendulo,
Izimpendul'ezingangiph'ukuthula,
Izimpendulo zemibuzo engapheli,
Izimpendulo ezingashabalalisa ukuzingabaza,
Kanti mina ngingubani?

Lingishonele mina kababa,
Ngisho izinyembei zigeleza ezinhlathini,
Ngisho ngifulathela,
Ngifulathela ngilambatha imibuzo imi mpo.
Kanti ngingubani?

Ithemba lishababalele,
Ngangithi goda ndini uyogqabuka langa libme,
Kant'angibuzang'elangeni,
Umhlaba ungehlule,
Ngivumile wethu, aphelile agambaqa.
Zozondini sesoye siye kagoqanyawo.

Translation: The shack

Heart, you ooze blood.
Luck, you have vanished.
Pains of the soul you are constant.
The flying termite is angry,
The flying termite overflows with hatred.
The arrow stabs without stop.

The one with a bad spirit is coming.
Death, you sting like a thorn.
Death, you tap the one who cries
Then you trap the one who hates.
Death, you hold secrets.
Though you cover me with pain I am still alive
And my heart will always say, ndo, ndo, ndo.

Steep hills stand dumb before the village rubbish heap,
Steep hills swallow the thorn that I have to extract from myself,
Steep hills conceal answers –
Answers that bring me no peace,
Answers to unending questions,
Answers that could stop me doubting myself:
Who am I?

The sun has gone down on me, oh, my God!
Tears flow down my cheeks!
Even when I have turned my back,
My back turned to the world and I am empty-handed,
Questions still stand firm:
Who am I?

Hope has vanished.
I thought the rope of companionship would never break
But I was fooling myself –
The world has defeated me!
I have run out of words,
There is nothing to gulp down.
Damn shack, we will end up dead.

Kanti Kungani

Ngivundulile ngadela,
Ngacinga ngakhathala,
Ngabuza ngibuzile
Kodwa aakukho naaaamunye onginike impendulo,
Kanti kungani?

Ummbele ugwansile,
Ubisi Alunathunga,
Pho, luzokwethelwaphi?
Ukuze luphenduke izaqheqhe
Ze sidle isizukulwane
Sishaye esentwala.

Thunga ndini utholwaphi?
Thunga ndini utholwa kanjani?
Thunga ndini utholwa obani?
Kanti Utholwa omtakabani yini?
Uma kungabanjalo,
Thina sosala sincela izithupa.

Ubusuku nemini ayabubuza amabhungezi
Ngithathe usiba nephepha ngilobe,
Ngilobe ngiphindelela,
Kepha izaqheqhe ziphela emilweni
Ngenxa yokweswela igula.
Kanti litholwa ngobani?

Ngicabangile ngokucwasana
Ngokwebala kodwa ngaphika.
Angithi zikhona izingwazi zakithi,
Ezetha eguleni lapho thina
Sishaye khona esentwala.

Kungani zingavuli amasango singene?
Kungani zingagqabuli amaketanga?
Thina sosishiyelani isizukulwane?
Ngobuza ngingaphezi ngithi – kanti kungani?

Translation: Why?

I have had enough of digging.
I searched, and was tired.
I asked and asked again,
But no one gave me the answer.
Why?

The cow's teat is full of milk
But there is no bucket,
So where are we going to store it?
Let it not turn to curds
Before the young generation can eat and finish up!

Milk-pail, where can we find you?
Milk-pail, how do we find you?
Milk-pail, who can find you?
Whose children will enjoy you?
If things go on like this
We shall be left sucking our thumbs.

Day and night wasps are buzzing.
I take pen and paper and write.
I write again and again
But curds end up in my fingers
Because I do not have the milk calabash.
Who can find it?

I thought about discriminating according to race
But disagreed.
We have our heroes who have the milk pail
Where we can guzzle.

Why don't they open the gate for us to enter?
Why are they not breaking these chains?
What are we going to leave for the generations to come?
I will not stop asking:
Why?

Uzifozonke

Umazi ngaliphi wena?
Umazelaphi kona?
Mina ngimazi ngomabizwasabele,
Mina ngimazi ngondlela zibukhali,
Ngiphinde ngimazi ngomkhunkuli wezinkinga.

Angithi ufika ihlangene phezulu
Eyomphefemulo edudulana ize iyongena
Shiqe emzimbeni, kushaye nhliziyo kushaye khanda,
Khuphukiyani, ushukela, kuxeg'amadolo.
Ngisho sewubona ukuthi likushonele,
Uzifo zonke ufika kube kanye.

Mbizandini ungenile imizi nemizana,
Ungena ntathakusa kushube,
Ungen'izinhlathi zigeleza izinyembezi,
Unyule umuntu egodini lokufa
Lapho umhlaba sewumehlule.

Uzwa ngandlebenye, ngelesithathu nqo.
Ngisho ntathakusa lapho kuphangelwana,
Angithi wonke umuntu ujahe ukophuza,
Basho bayihudule odade nabafo.
Zishe izikhotha, lushunqe uthuli.

Angithi phela isuke sebeyigovuz'imbiza,
Nabondodensth'emaflethini, omam'oright.
Obayidudile, ngisho nonk'otime to time.
Beyititinya behosha nayo ongqalabutho.
Ngingabaceda ngithini?

Inhliziyo igeleze intokozo,
Kuqhubuke izihlathi,
Injabulo ikhephukis'okwegwebu'
Angith'uzifo zonke ufikile?
Ngomkhohlwa ngifile.

Translation: The plague

By what name do you know him?
From where do you know him?
I know him as the one who responds when called,
I know him as a thorny road.
I also know him as the one who casts spells.

He arrives when the spirit pushes
Until it enters and gathers on top.
When there is heartache and headache
Up goes sugar diabetes, weakening the knees.
Even when the sun has gone down on you
This plague comes.

Damn pot, you have besieged big and small houses!
You besieged at dawn causing bitterness!
You besiege leaving cheeks flowing with tears!
You visit a person in the pit of death
When the world has defeated him.

At three o'clock you hear with one ear.
At dawn when people are rushing,
When everyone is in a hurry to drink,
Young men and women drag you,
Veld burns, dust dances.

It is when they stir the pot,
Guys and girls at the flats,
Bands of disturbers, I mean all of you,
From time to time,
And examining him closely, also the warriors.
I cannot count all of them!

My heart flows with happiness
And my cheeks glow.
Joy foams over –
The plague has arrived!
Will I forget him when I am dead?

Anna Anuradhá Varney

Alchemy

at first a small flame flickered
now I build a sacred cauldron
to contain this molten force
I feed the furnace
with embers from the heart

hush
have no fear
this fire does not consume
it burns clean
there is no harm

For Gra-anna
(1979 – 2004)

my candle burns for you
incense swirls through in the air

your words once so clear
so wilful & passionate
now in dreams
you speak in signs
& so I look for signs
finding them everywhere;
stars, praying mantises,
feathers, roses, flying birds

my darling child
this pain I carry
this treasure is mine
I look back over my shoulder
wailing into eternity
I smile too
2 headed
as the sun breaks through
I reach forward
nurturing those who stayed behind

my beloved
our chord
still intact
you are still mine
softly under my healing love
I hold a candle
looking out for you
at last transcending this hardship
you are so radiant
building a temple

I receive initiations
I am building my love
an archway will meet
from both sides
of the veil

Measured

Inexhaustible
streams of cobalt
where lights sparkle
His eyes seem to restore me

Then
he picks up a measuring tape:
"This is the parameter
of the universe"

From my belly
comes the response:
Eternity
has no length
no breadth.
Only the snippets
we snip

Torn fabric

Binding us to conflict

End of a cycle

When I look back I cannot remember
the beginning of it all.
Beasts have roamed free
and preyed off babes.
Storms raged ceaselessly,
creating such catastrophe.
Mothers buried their children
& gathered survivors to their breasts
where the last of the sun shone

I rode that raging storm
till I could bear no more.
Found a desolate landscape.
Felt I could rest there
in that place of bones.
Everything subsiding at last.
Endless silence

But a hand broke through
that inert sky
to lead me back.
This journey I'm meant to take.

Slowly   slowly   I find the eye
of the storm
& lay myself down

Sea Point

raucously
we eat our dinner
discussing seagull chicks
who run along roof ledges
– but never quite fall over

we ignore the gulls scream
at midnight
– they who yell and squawk
over lit street lamps
having sacrificed
sleep
for a life
of our crumbs

Divine Kali

Kali, Kali, Kali,
how to experience you with grace?
Beloved Kali

Those who quake in your presence
who weep because their feet are torn
don't see the beauty in your dark form
they do not understand
that skulls & ash give way
to the piercing scream
of a woman in labour

seasons change
change always

Kali: Hindu goddess often associated with evil & death
    but is the embodiment of Mother Nature and natural cycles

There is no choice

I meet this risk willingly
I have no choice

perhaps at some distant crossroads
long before we were born
long before the dream
then
perhaps
then
there was choice

Sacred Yoni

I watch the scarlet droplet
fall
just as thrilled as the 1st time
– this Woman-Being experience

It's pain pain pain
ocean deep
deep
me in the depths
where light cannot reach
out of reach
beyond where I'll see tomorrow
behind the mind
where the Sorceress dwells

Yoni: (Sanskrit) Source; womb, female genital organs

A piece of jazz

1

it's after five
people in a taxi line
each made art this morning
when they dressed
just look at that picture!

2

a walking constellation
of EVERYTHING
this man is selling EVERYTHING
dangling from EVERYWHERE
an assemblage
not a mistake
by design
organic clown earth design

Notes written on the train in Mossel Bay

1
Women screech
below in the dark
all undone
+ I think I may be
far too gathered
I tell my baby
I'm 'a clever'

2
Out in the bay
ourange-outang spiders
cling to a small grey
fishing boat

3
The plump woman
in the red jersey
walks ahead of the man
she colours her hair
he leaves his thin
and grey

She turns treading backwards
she pulls him in

4
A couple stand
on the beach back to back
yin and yang

he steps away
to face her
with his camera

she's an arc
head turned demurely
toward the sea

Prayer

Forgive me for my efforts.
As though my gross actions
can in any way improve
Your perfect song!
I should just sit here
in an eternal lotus
listening to Your melody

I give thanks for all
You do to help me
that my efforts
become effortless

Selection

As with a flipped coin;
only one side
of the whole
is possible here

Anna Anuradhá Varney

Biographies

elsbeth e lives in Cape Town and works at the Surplus Peoples Project; she is involved in rural development in Namaqualand.

Sumeera Dawood has crawled out from beneath her camouflaged rock, plopped out a few short poems, and crawled back lazily towards her rock with a stash of bitter chocolate, a brand new kitten and a mounted stuffed earlobe trophy. She's 25, and the online editor at a small, Cape Town based publishing house.

Lisemelo Tlale was born in the Free State. She spent several years in Cape Town working as an information technology officer for a clothing company. She is currently living in Europe.

Elizabeth Trew returned to South Africa in 1991 after many years in exile, teaches English language at Wits and is a gender activist and volunteer counsellor with People Opposed to Women Abuse (POWA). She has published in magazines in South Africa and England.

Anet Kemp was born in the Free State and now lives in Pietermaritzburg. She has a Masters degree in the field of literary criticism and has published poems and articles on literary and art history topics. She teaches, edits and does translations and is currently working on more poetry as well as a novel.

Baitse Mokiti was born in 1978 in Soweto and still lives in Johannesburg. She is a freelance media worker and was active in the Bla©k Pen literary group.

Myesha Jenkins was born in 1948; she works in community development and is a regular at jazz clubs, bookstores and friends' kitchens in and around Jozi. She began writing poems after immigrating to South Africa from the USA in 1993. Her poetry has appeared in journals and magazines and was featured in *Insight* (Timbila). Her new solo collection is entitled *Breaking the Surface* (Timbila). She has performed her poetry on radio and TV and was a founding member of the Feela Sistah! Spoken Word Collective.

Arja Salafranca was born in Spain but has lived in South Africa since the age of five. Her first poetry collection, *A life stripped of illusions*, received the 1994 Sanlam Award for poetry, a short story, *Couple on the Beach* was a winner of the same award in 1999 for short fiction. Her second collection of poetry, *The fire in which we burn*, was published in 2000. Arja has worked for various newspapers in Johannesburg and now edits the Sunday Life supplement in The Sunday Independent.

Makhosazana Xaba was born in 1957. She grew up in Ndaleni and currently lives in Jozi. She is a feminist specializing in Women's Health. Her debut poetry book *these hands* was published by Timbila in January 2005.

Riana Wiechers is a 31-year old language practitioner and freelance writer living in Cape Town. Pastimes include reading, writing, music, photography and dreaming about one day having the time and self-discipline to write a book.

Bongekile Mbanjwa lives in Pietermaritzburg. She has worked for various social welfare organizations including the KwaZulu-Natal Society for the Blind.

Anna Anuradhá Varney was born in 1959 and lives in Johannesburg. She is a yoga teacher, graphic designer and artist. Her poems and essays have been published in *We Jive Like This*, *Dirty Washing* (Botsotso Publishing), *Like A House on Fire* (COSAW), Botsotso Magazine, Timbila and other literary journals. She has been a member of the Botsotso Jesters and her performance poetry is featured on the CD, *Purple Light Mirror in the Mud*.

Suzy Bernstein lives in Johannesburg. She has been involved in photography since the late 1980's. When she is not working on commissions, she does personal work. Photography, for her, is a constant source of inspiration and an exhilarating way in which to explore the world.

Neo Ntsoma is a 32yr old female photographer based in Johannesburg. When growing up her interest was in film and television, but because of race restrictions at the time, she could not fulfil her wish. Between 1992 and 1994 she received photography training at Peninsula Technikon in Cape Town and Tshwane University of Technology in Pretoria. She then freelanced for two and half years in Mmabatho before moving to Johannesburg to work as a freelance photojournalist with various newspapers and magazines (The Star, Sunday Times and several magazines). Her work has been published in many international publications as well as being exhibited.

Allan Kolski Horwitz was born in 1952 and grew up in Cape Town where he studied political philosophy and literature. He currently works for a social housing association and member-controlled provident fund in Johannesburg. He is the coordinator of the Botsotso Jesters and Botsotso Publishing. His first book of poems *Call from the Free State* was published in 1979. Substantial selections of his poetry have been included in *Essential Things* (COSAW, 1992) and *Throbbing Ink* (Timbila, 2003) as well as the various Botsotso publications. His fiction has been included in two collections, *Unity in Flight* (2001) and *Un/common Ground* (2002).

BOTSOTSO PUBLISHING TITLES

Annual Literary Journal/Magazine

BOTSOTSO

Poetry

WE JIVE LIKE THIS   Botsotso Jesters
(Siphiwe ka Ngwenya, Isabella Motadinyane, Allan Kolski Horwitz, Ike Mboneni Muila, Anna Anuradhá Varney)

NO FREE SLEEPING
Donald Parenzee, Vonani wa ka Bila, Alan Finlay

DIRTY WASHING   Botsotso Jesters

PURPLE LIGHT MIRROR IN THE MUD (CD)
Botsotso Jesters & Lionel Murcott (Music – James de Villiers)

5
Clinton du Plessis, Kobus Moolman, Gillian Schutte, Mphutlane wa Bofelo, Lionel Murcott

GOVA   Ike Mboneni Muila

GREETINGS EMSAWAWA   Botsotso Jesters

SOUL FIRE EXPERIENCE   Siphiwe ka Ngwenya

Short Fiction

UNITY IN FLIGHT
Maropodi Mapalakanye, Peter Rule, Zachariah Rapola, Michael Vines, Phaswane Mpe, Allan Kolski Horwitz

UN/COMMON GROUND   Allan Kolski Horwitz

POST-TRAUMATIC   Edited: Chris van Wyk

JAIL BIRDS AND OTHERS   Muthal Naidoo

Art

MANUSCRIPT EXHIBITION 2000   Anna Anuradhá Varney

MANUSCRIPT EXHIBITION 2002   Anna Anuradhá Varney